£1-50

DOCUMENTS OF SOCIAL HISTORY
Editor: Anthony Adams

A MEMOIR OF EDMUND CARTWRIGHT

A MEMOIR
OF
EDMUND CARTWRIGHT

WITH AN INTRODUCTION BY
Kenneth G. Ponting

ADAMS & DART

First published in 1843
This edition published in 1971
for Social Documents Ltd
by Adams & Dart, 40 Gay Street, Bath, Somerset
SBN 239 00084 6
Printed in Great Britain by Redwood Press Ltd,
Trowbridge and London

EDMUND CARTWRIGHT

Amongst textile inventors Edmund Cartwright occupies a distinguished place, and no one has ever questioned the importance of the part he played in the invention of power loom weaving and machine combing. The many questions that have been raised over the rival claims of Paul and Wyatt, of Arkwright and Highs, in machine spinning do not find a parallel here, perhaps because of their different backgrounds. Whereas most other textile inventors of the eighteenth century were men engaged in the industry – Lewis Paul appears to be an exception – Cartwright had no connections at all with the industry. Indeed, with his clerical background he has more parallels with that great knitting genius, William Lee of Calverton.

Moreover, Cartwright has other claims to fame. In the field of inventions he had patents on ropemaking, bricks, indestructible materials for dwelling houses, and steam engines. He was also a poet whose early work, 'Armina and Elvira: A Legendary Tale', went through several editions, and although now usually dismissed as almost unreadable, it has a certain interest as representing a slight breakaway from eighteenth-century traditions. Perhaps more interesting is his friendship with several of the most eminent men of his day. His brother, Major John Cartwright (1740–1824) was an important parliamentary reformer; from the first he supported the American colonists' fight for independence, and later in England his great task was the achievement of universal suffrage and annual parliaments. The idea of political associations led to the famous Corresponding Societies. Major Cartwright worked unceasingly for political reform and has indeed been well praised for it, notably by M. Halevy, who considered him the founder of English radicalism. There is little sign that Edmund gave his brother much support in his political activities, but John certainly shared in Edmund's industrial ventures. Other friends were equally distinguished. Sir Walter Scott thought well of 'Armina and Elvira', but his most interesting literary friend was George Crabbe, several of whose letters are included in this volume, and who said of Cartwright: 'Few persons could tell a good story so well, no man could make more of a trite one . . . I can just remember him, the portly, dignified old gentleman of the last generation, grave and polite, his face full of humour and spirit'.

Bearing these many qualities in mind, it is strange that there has been no modern biography of Cartwright. The volume here reprinted is rare and difficult to obtain and gives a very readable account of his life, and is particularly important for the selection of his own writings and of letters he received. The original 1843 edition is called *A Memoir of the Life, Writings and Mechanical Inventions of Edmund Cartwright*, with no mention of the author or editor, but all the copies the present writer has seen have either the initials M.S. or the fuller M. Strickland, and it is known that this family was connected with the Cartwrights.

Margaret Strickland was the sister of Agnes Strickland, the prolific writer about royalty whose lives of the Queens of England do, however, contain valuable original material. Margaret wrote a life of her sister and a book on Rome, and a short life of her appears in the *Dictionary of National Biography*.

To turn now to Cartwright's two major inventions, the best account of the power loom is contained in a letter he wrote to a Mr Ballantyne, author of the article 'Cotton Manufacture' in the first edition of the *Encyclopaedia Britannica*, and as Margaret Strickland does not quote it the reader may find it useful to have the text:

'Happening to be at Matlock in the summer of 1784, I fell in company with some gentlemen of Manchester, when our conversation turned on Arkwright's spinning machine. One of the company observed that as soon as Arkwright's patent expired so many mills would be erected and so much cotton spun that hands could never be found to weave it. To this observation I replied that Arkwright must set his wits to work then to invent a weaving mill. This brought on a conversation on the subject, in which the Manchester gentlemen unanimously agreed that the thing was impracticable; and, in defence of their opinion, they adduced arguments which I certainly was incompetent to answer or even to comprehend, being totally ignorant of the subject having never, at that time, seen a person weave. I controverted, however, the impracticability of the thing by remarking that there had lately been exhibited in London an automatic figure which played at chess. Now you will not assert gentlemen, said I, that it is more difficult to construct a machine that shall weave than one that shall make all the variety of moves which are required in that complicated game.

Some time afterwards a particular circumstance recalling this conversation to my mind, it struck me that as in plain weaving, according to the conception I then had of the business, there could only be three movements which were to follow each other in succession, there would be little difficulty in reproducing and repeating them. Full of these ideas I immediately employed a carpenter and smith to carry them into effect. As soon as the machine was finished I got a weaver to put in the warp which was of such material as sail cloth is usually made of. To my great delight

7

a piece of cloth, such as it was, was the produce. As I never before had turned my thoughts to anything mechanical, either in theory or practice, nor had ever seen a loom at work or knew anything of its construction, you will readily suppose that my first loom was a most rude piece of machinery. The warp was placed perpendicularly, the reed fell with at least the weight of half a hundredweight, and the springs which threw the shuttle were strong enough to have thrown a Congreive rocket. In short, it required the strength of two powerful men to work the machine at a slow rate and only for a short time. Conceiving in my simplicity that I had accomplished all that was required, I then secured what I thought a most valuable property by a patent dated 4th April, 1785. This being done, I condescended to see how other people wove, and you may guess my astonishment when I compared their easy mode of operation with mine. Availing myself, however, of what I then saw, I made a loom in its general principles nearly as they are now made. But it was not until the year 1787 that I completed my invention when I took out my weaving patent on August 1st of that year.'

It is interesting to compare this account of an invention with the many years' work that was necessary, for example, to evolve the Sulzer weaving machine in this century, the first loom that really made a successful break from the power loom as originated by Cartwright.

Cartwright's second loom was very different from the first. It was no longer perpendicular, for having studied the hand loom he had realised that although there may only be three basic motions no loom, particularly a power loom, could work without a number of auxiliary ones. For example, the point at which the beat up motion would meet the already woven cloth will change every pick unless some automatic device was fitted to the loom that allowed the warp to be run off and the newly woven cloth wound up after each pick. Due to the constantly changing size of the beams (that is, containers) in question, this was no easy job. Some arrangement must be added so that the loom stops if the weft breaks. In his second loom Cartwright added these motions plus others, such as a warp-stop motion if the warp breaks, and a system for sizing the warp. The warp-stop motion is not essential and the sizing is better done before the warp goes in the loom. Cartwright had gone from one extreme to another, from having too few motions he now had too many. Further improvements, however, did produce a loom that worked. Cartwright had proved his point, but his power loom was not widely adopted and the inventor decided to go into business himself. However, his Doncaster venture was a failure, and Cartwright then lost interest in his power loom.

It is worth commenting that it took the cotton trade a further twenty-five years and the wool trade a further fifty years to really adopt the power loom, partly because as left by Cartwright it did need further improvements, but mainly, I feel, because an innate conservatism led people to believe that the hand loom would stay for ever.

In many ways Cartwright's other major textile invention is even more interesting. Whereas with weaving, after his first highly individual effort, he really only applied power to what was basically a hand loom, with combing he had to originate. There was no way in which the old hand process of combing could be simply mechanised. His invention has been well described in two nineteenth-century books on textiles, *The History of Worsted Manufacturing* by J. James, and *The History of Wool and Wool Combing* by James Burnley. He realised that any mechanised form of combing

9

had to be circular in concept, but unfortunately he embodied this important idea in rather a clumsy machine, so much so that it was called Big Ben after the name of a famous prizefighter of the time. In all he took out three patents, and his machine was used with some success for coarse wool, but as far as fine wool combing was concerned the hand methods held their own for almost another fifty years. It required a great deal of work by such men as Heilmann of Mulhose in Alsace, and of Holden and Donisthorpe in England, combined with the entrepreneur Lister, to finally produce a completely satisfactory machine.

Most of Cartwright's inventive work in textiles was accomplished before 1800. Thereafter, as Margaret Strickland says, his lack of perseverance and tendency to flit from one idea to another gained in strength, but his work at Woburn, his friendship with Robert Fulton, are typical of the man and show him experimenting to the end. Cartwright had undertaken the management of the Duke of Bedford's model farm at Woburn in 1801, and it was there that he met Robert Fulton, an important American engineer famous as the first man to make steam navigation practical. They became great friends, and Cartwright constructed a small steamboat which, for a time, plied on the pond at Woburn.

Finally, towards the end of his long life, Cartwright realised that he had greatly impoverished himself by his desultory speculations and inventive pursuits. In 1808, therefore, he petitioned Parliament for some pecuniary recognition of his inventive gifts to the industry of the nation. Though he claimed to have spent £30,000 on the power loom alone, Parliament could not be brought to grant so great a sum for any industrial achievement. He was, however, granted £10,000 in recognition of the great service he had rendered to the public by his invention of machine weaving. This reward can be reckoned reasonably generous in comparison with the £5,000 that was given to Crompton, whose mule certainly had a far greater effect on spinning than Cartwright's power loom had on weaving.

A MEMOIR

OF

THE LIFE, WRITINGS,

AND

Mechanical Inventions,

OF

EDMUND CARTWRIGHT,

D.D. F.R.S.,

INVENTOR OF THE POWER LOOM,

ETC. ETC.

LONDON

SAUNDERS AND OTLEY, CONDUIT STREET.

1843.

PREFACE.

The following Memoir of the Life of Dr. Cartwright, being chiefly derived from authentic papers in the possession of his family, and also from the personal recollection of its few surviving members, will be found to contain a more connected account than has hitherto appeared of the various pursuits of his long and useful life. It might have been considerably extended by the addition of interesting letters from various eminent persons with whom he had correspondence; but the Author has preferred making such selections only as seem connected with the leading points of Dr. Cartwright's character and history.

The mechanical portions of this little work might also have been made more copious; but the minuteness of detail necessary to render such descriptions intelligible would have but little interest to the general reader. If, therefore, this volume deserve the censure of being meagre as well as short, it may hope at least to escape the heavier reproach of being tedious and diffuse.

M. S.

CONTENTS.

CHAPTER I.

CHAPTER II.

CHAPTER III.

CONTENTS.

CHAPTER IV.

CHAPTER V.

CHAPTER VI.

CHAPTER VII.

CHAPTER VIII.

CONTENTS.

CHAPTER IX.

Correspondence with Dr. Bardsley — Locomotive carriage—Theory of the planetary system—Explosive engine — Declining health — Decease — Dr. Bardsley's letter to S. Oldknow, Esq.

APPENDIX.

MEMOIR

ETC.

CHAPTER I.

IN contemplating the wonderful impulse
which the manufactures of Great Britain
have received within the last fifty years,
from an unprecedented application of mechanical ingenuity, the mind is led not only
to inquire into the causes that have produced such a direction of talent, but naturally awakened to an interest in the history
of those enterprising men who, in departing
from immemorial practice, first gave that
impulse, and prepared the way, through dif-

ficulties and opposition, for the more pros-
perous career of their successors.

Some of the most original mechanicians
of the eighteenth century were persons born
in very humble stations of life. In poverty
and obscurity, they encountered such impe-
diments to their successful progress, as the
force of native talent alone could not overcome; and their history but too often presents a melancholy picture of the unavailing
struggles of a vigorous mind, subdued at
length by the mortification of seeing others
enriched by inventions which the author of
them possessed not the means to introduce.

The subject of the following memoir cannot be said to come within the same description of unfortunate projectors; but though
possessed of advantages which supported
him through difficulties under which an
humbler individual might have sunk, he was

not the less-exposed to the influence of that spirit of jealousy which has a tendency not only to oppose every new invention, but to dispute with the inventor his claim to originality. It is solely in the hope of doing full justice to the memory of so ingenious a man as Dr. Cartwright that these pages are offered to the public. Several years have now elapsed since his death, and as the number is daily diminishing of those whose personal recollection can throw any light on the earlier portion of his mechanical career, the very few who still survive are anxious to shew the ground on which he claimed the merit of being the original inventor of certain combinations in machinery, which, from their extensive adoption, have had no small influence on the commercial and manufacturing interests of this country. But, before any explanation or description be given of inventions that have produced most important results, or the circumstances related, which called his mechanical genius into action, a slight sketch of the pursuits and habits of his earlier life may not be uninteresting, in order to shew that, however intellectual they might be, they were not apparently calculated to develop the peculiar talent by which his later years were distinguished.

It is now precisely a century since the birth of Edmund Cartwright, on the 24th April, 1743. He was the fourth son of William Cartwright, Esq., of Marnham, in the county of Nottingham, by Anne, daughter of George Cartwright, Esq., of Ossington, in the same county.* He was educated

---

* The family of Cartwright had been long established in Nottinghamshire. From the three sons of Hugh Cartwright, in the time of Henry VII., de-

under Dr. Clarke, at the grammar-school at Wakefield, where he was early distinguished for proficiency in his studies. Had he been permitted to follow the bent of his own inclination in the choice of a profession, he would have preferred the navy; but two of his brothers being already designed for that service, it was thought advisable that Edmund should apply what were justly consi-

scended the families of Cartwright of Marnham, (originally of Norwell,) of Ayho, in the county of Northampton, and of Ossington. Frequent intermarriages had taken place between the two families of Marnham and Ossington, both of whom had suffered in their fortunes by their adherence to the cause of Charles the First. The Ossington branch became extinct in the male line in George Cartwright, Esq., who died in 1762, leaving four daughters (Mary, married to Sir Charles Buck, Bart.; Dorothy, to Henry, Lord Middleton; Jane, to Sir Digby Legard; and Anne, to Sir John Whiteford, Bart.), by whom the estate at Ossington was sold to William Dennison, Esq.

dered as promising abilities to one of the
learned professions; and as his family connexions might be expected to promote his
advancement in the church, it was decided
by his parents that he should enter into
holy orders. He began his academical
studies at University College, in Oxford,
where he was entered at fourteen years of
age, and during the vacations was placed
under the private tuition of the Rev. Dr.
Langhorne, a name well known in the literary world, as the editor of Plutarch's Lives,
and likewise as the author of some poems,
as well as several pleasing and elegant volumes in prose.

A friendship, honourable to both, seems
to have arisen between the pupil and his in-
structor, to whose classical knowledge and
literary taste Dr. Cartwright might probably be indebted for much of that neat and

finished style of expression which he employed in writing, even on the most trivial and familiar occasions.

At that period, the chief object of a liberal education was to acquire a competent portion of classical learning; and he who added a taste for poetry and the belles lettres to his proficiency as a scholar, could not fail of being distinguished as possessing more than an ordinary share of the attainments that were then most valued in polished society. Much of what is considered as general information was not always to be found even amongst well educated persons, and scientific studies were comparatively but little cultivated. Had those various sources of information been then accessible which are now within the reach of every one who can read, or those popular associations existed, which, by uniting the results of inquiring minds, serve at once to concentrate knowledge and diffuse practical instruction, it is more than probable that the peculiar bent of Dr. Cartwright's genius would have sooner shewn itself, and that he would have aimed rather at reaping the fruits of science than culling the flowers of poetry. It seemed, however, to have been the natural, as it was the not unusual resource of the young and vigorous mind, to relieve its aspirations after distinction by an assiduous cultivation of the muses. Nor was such a dedication of the youthful faculties in this instance to be regretted. The occasional composition of poetry became to him, in after life, a frequent solace under disappointments, and contributed, with other mental exercises, to promote that cheerfulness of spirit, for which, even in his most advanced age, Dr. Cartwright was re-

markable. That he had become a votary
of the muses at the early age of eighteen is
inferred from a letter, dated September 1761,
from an old friend, Dr. Hasledine, rector of
Haceby, in Lincolnshire, in which he says,
" I presume your muse is very busy at this
time, and I shall be glad to see your name
in the collection of verses now preparing on
the king's* wedding." Whether the youthful
poet adopted his friend's suggestion, in
adding to the numerous loyal effusions which
so propitious an occasion could not fail to
produce, cannot now be ascertained; but in
the following spring he appears to have
committed some of his compositions to the
press, as well as submitted them to the
criticism of his learned and affectionate
tutor, Dr. Langhorne, who, in a letter,
dated February 1762, thus expresses his

* George III.

opinion of the juvenile performance of his pupil:—"I rejoice to find that, though you have long neglected your muse, she has not taken a final leave of you. Many of your verses are pretty; but I am less pleased with the harmony of your little poem than with that philosophical temper you seem to have been in when you wrote it—' *Sunt lachrymæ rerum et mentem mortalia tangunt.* '" His brother John, (afterwards Major Cartwright,) then a lieutenant on board H.M.S. " Wasp," in a letter, dated 1763, also alludes to his poetical attempts, and draws an interesting comparison between his own neglected education and his brother Edmund's superior advantages in that respect:—

" I shall beg you will indulge me with a sight of some of those little pieces, in the composition of which you sometimes amuse yourself. Give me leave to inform you that I already rank one poet amongst my intimate correspondents, (and he* of no small note either,) so you need not be shy of not getting into good company. It is my ambition to converse with the geniuses (if I may not write genii) of the age,—and learned men I honour exceedingly. Were I a potentate, they should be respected at my court before nobles, and it should be glorious from the lustre of their wisdom. Though my soil was under the care of slothful husbandmen, and has been denied the sunshine of a college; though it has also been for several seasons exposed to ruthless, inclement elements—the most inveterate enemies to erudition; yet do not altogether consider the produce of a richer one, that has had a happier cultivation be-

* Falconer, author of the " Shipwreck."

stowed upon it, as pearls cast before swine."
It appears from the following letter, that,
although Mr. Cartwright had determined
on publishing some of his poetical effusions,
he had, at the same time, a youthful
anxiety not to be known as their author.

FROM DR. LANGHORNE.

"Feb. 1764.

" MY DEAR CARTWRIGHT,—In consequence
of your letter, received this morning, I
travelled through a terrible shower of rain,
to the printer of the ' Monthly Review,' in
order to scratch out your name and the
name of your college. It is done, sir, and
you are now a bare blank, or what, perhaps,
you may like better, four stars. Magdalen*
College is indeed mentioned in the latter
sonnet; but that is nothing to you, it being

---

* Mr. Cartwright had been elected a Fellow of
Magdalen College, Oxford.

only introduced as the nurse of Addison and Collins. * * * But what! are you going to turn Dutch commentator, and give us a new edition of old Politian's old letters? Really, my friend, for your green time of life, this appears to me *mal-àpropos*, however wise or however learned your sage adviser may be. Had you proposed to give a translation of Politian, with notes, the public might have been the better for it, and you, too, possibly, might have had some reward for your labours; but to dig in the Bentleyan mine with your young muscles, I own, appears absurd to me, and will surely gain you no other character in your university than that of a prig."

In 1770, Mr. Cartwright published "Armine and Elvira," a legendary tale. This poem, which passed through several editions in little more than a year, was greatly ad-

mired for the harmony of its numbers and
the purity of its moral sentiment, and the
author received compliments from various
quarters sufficient to have satisfied the
vanity of a much vainer man; but " The
Prince of Peace," an ode, published in the
year 1779, must unquestionably be considered as the best of his earlier poetical
productions, probably for this reason, that
he *felt* his subject. The deep regret with
which, in common with many others of the
wise and good, he viewed the contest at
that time subsisting between Great Britain
and her American colonies, seems to have
inspired his pen, and deprecating the mode
in which the warfare was carried on, he describes its horrors in some very noble lines.
The concluding stanzas of a poem out of
print, and now but little known, may not
be unacceptable to the reader :—

" Ah! surely dead to human woe
    Their iron hearts, that deeds like these approve!
All future hope they surely must forego,
    Nor fear a vindicating Power above :
And yet—to Heaven they bow the suppliant
       knee,
    And breathe the formal prayer with lips defiled ;
And yet—they lift their blood-stain'd hands to
       Thee,
    To Thee, meek SAVIOUR, merciful and mild !
And yet—to Thee those hands they DARE to shew !
To Thee, who didst COMMAND affection to the foe.

Thou Friend of Man ! at Pity's call,
    Once more thy Spirit in their hearts renew !
And oh may Heaven, whose mercy stoops to all,
    Their crimes forgive !—they know not what
       they do !
In rival breasts awake thy law of love !
    From Thee all human hope, all comfort, springs !
The mutual wound's keen anguish to remove,
    Arise once more, with healing on thy wings !
So may each doubt dissolve, all discord cease,
And kindred nations bow before the PRINCE OF
    PEACE."

No one was more ready than Mr. Cartwright to acknowledge and admire the superior power of some of our later poets; and when, at a very advanced age, he took a pleasure in accounting himself the father of the living poets, he gave a pleasing instance of his candour in a letter to one of them,* which it may not be irrelevant to introduce in this place. "You have, it seems, made repeated incursions into Parnassus, and so have I—*in Arcadia ego*, that is to say, about half a century ago. You probably are not aware of the relationship in which we stand; having been the father of the living poets for many years past, you consequently are one of my poetical sons. No poetical father, there is reason to believe, ever had so numerous or so illustrious

* Mr. James Montgomery.

a family before. When I first appeared in the poetical horizon, there were scarcely a dozen poets, good or bad: now they are as numerous as the stars of heaven; the greater part shining, not with borrowed light, as formerly, but with original splendour. You will most likely be at a loss to know how I make myself out to be the patriarch of the English Parnassus. I date my poetical paternity from the year 1762, when I first appeared in print. Not many years afterwards I published "Armine and Elvira," a legendary tale, which went through seven editions in little more than a year, at a time when few of my poetical sons now living could have held a pen, or probably were born."*

* In the Essay on Imitations of the Ancient Ballad, (written in 1830,) prefixed to the third part of "Minstrelsy of the Scottish Border," Sir Walter

In 1772, Mr. Cartwright married Alice,
the youngest daughter and co-heiress of
Richard Whitaker, Esq., of Doncaster, and,
after his marriage, resided first at Marnham,
and afterwards at Brampton, in Derbyshire,
to the perpetual curacy of which he was

Scott bears the following testimony to the poetical
merit of " Armine and Elvira :"—

" We need only stop to mention another very
beautiful piece of this fanciful kind, by Dr. Cartwright, called ' Armine and Elvira,' containing
some excellent poetry, expressed with unusual felicity. I have a vision of having met this accomplished gentleman in my very early youth, and am
the less likely to be mistaken, as he was the first
living poet I recollect to have seen.* His poem had

---

* " If I am right in what must be a very early
recollection, I saw Mr. Cartwright (then a student
of medicine at the Edinburgh University) at the
house of my maternal grandfather, John Ruther-
ford, M.D."

presented by the Dean of Lincoln, Dr. Cust. He still continued his correspondence with his old friend, Dr. Langhorne, who in a letter, dated from Blagden, near Bristol, expresses himself in the following affectionate manner.

the distinguished honour to be much admired by our celebrated philosopher, Dugald Stewart, who was wont to quote, with much pathos, the picture of resignation in the following stanza :—

> 'And while his eye to heaven he raised,
>   Its silent waters stole away.'"

It is hardly necessary to remark the slight mistake relative to Mr. Cartwright's early pursuits. He never was a student of medicine at any university.

In some modern periodical work, along with a contemptuous notice of "Armine and Elvira," it has been erroneously stated that Dr. Cartwright was the author of several novels. There is not the least reason to believe that he ever wrote a novel in his life.

" I rejoice in your letter for many reasons. You might, for aught I had learnt to the contrary, have been these twenty months in the number of those Sacerdotes casti (Æn. VI. 661), who, a sone of our prophets hath spoken, wear white ribbons, and sing songs, and dine upon a grass plot surrounded with bays, at the head of the great river Eridanus. Seriously, I was a very little while since apprehensive that you were on the road before me. Amongst the arrivals at the Hotwells, I saw a Reverend Mr. Cartwright, and having never heard of any other person of that denomination, I set off from hence to Bristol, with a melancholy mind, to satisfy the most painful kind of curiosity I ever felt. I passed with horror, literally speaking, through the shades, such were the objects I saw creeping to and from the pump, and felt certainly more satisfaction in not finding a friend than I ever have known, or ever shall know, in meeting him. So much for your existence, which, if it be in any tolerable state, is a material point. Your poetical being can neither be doubted nor feared. When you favour me again, I wish you to domesticate a little. Tell me where, in what manner, and upon what, you live. I should be extremely happy in the indulgence of a hope that our never broken, though often interrupted friendship, might devolve to our little boys, and should have pleasure in concerting with you the means of promoting it; but * * * * * 'The grim fury with the abhorred shears.' I beg you will present my most respectful compliments to Mrs. E. C., Lady Tyrconnel, and the rest of the Marnham family, and believe me, ever yours,

" J. LANGHORNE."

During Mr. Cartwright's residence in Derbyshire, he made the discovery of a remedy of considerable efficacy in cases of putrid fever. The parish of Brampton was of considerable extent, the inhabitants very poor, and medical assistance frequently out of their reach. With a view to relieve the distresses of his parishioners, he applied himself to the study of medical books, and was often enabled to give advice, not the less welcome for being gratuitous. Of the circumstances that first led to the trial of yeast as a remedy for putrid fever, the following relation, published in a medical work of the year 1799, is from his own pen:—

" During my residence, upwards of twenty years ago, at Brampton, a populous parish near Chesterfield, a putrid fever broke out amongst us. Finding by far the greater number of my parishioners too poor to afford themselves medical assistance, I undertook, by the help of such books on the subject of medicine as were within my possession, to prescribe for them. I attended a boy of about fourteen years of age who was attacked by the fever. He had not been ill many days before the symptoms were unequivocally putrid. I then administered bark, wine, and such other medicines as my books directed. My exertions were, however, of no avail; his disorder grew every day more and more untractable and malignant, so that I was in hourly expectation of his dissolution. Being under the necessity of taking a journey, before I set off, I went to see him, as I thought, for the last time; and I prepared his parents for the event of his death, which I considered as inevitable, and reconciled them in the best manner I was able to a loss which I knew they would feel severely. While I was in conversation on this distressing subject with his mother, I observed in a corner of the room a small tub of wort working. The sight brought to my recollection an experiment I had somewhere met with, of a piece of putrid meat being made sweet by being suspended over a tub of wort in the act of fermentation. The idea flashed into my mind that the yeast might correct the putrid nature of the disease, and I instantly gave him two large spoonfuls. I then told the mother if she found her son better to repeat this dose every two hours. I then set out on my journey. Upon my return, after a few days, I anxiously inquired after the boy, and was informed that he was recovered. I could not repress my curiosity, and though greatly fatigued with my journey, and night was come on, I went directly to his residence, which was three miles off, in a wild part of the moors, and to my great surprise the boy himself opened the door, looking well, and he told me he had felt better from the time he took the yeast.

" After I left Brampton, I lived in Leicestershire. My parishioners there being few and opulent, I dropped the medical character entirely, and would not prescribe for my own family. One of my domestics falling ill, the apothecary was sent for. Having great reliance, and deservedly, on the apothecary's* skill and judgment, the man was left entirely to his management. His disorder, however, kept gaining ground, and the apothecary finding himself baffled in every attempt to be of service to him, told

* Mr. Whitchurch, of Melton Mowbray.

me he considered it to be a lost case, and in his opinion the man could not live twenty-four hours. On this, I determined to try the effects of yeast. I gave him two large spoonfuls, and in fifteen minutes from taking the yeast, his pulse, though still feeble, began to get composed and full. In thirty-two minutes from his taking it, he was able to get up from his bed. The expression that he made use of to describe the effect to his own feelings was, that he felt ' quite lightsome.' At the expiration of the second hour, I gave him sago, with wine and ginger, &c., and in another hour repeated the yeast. An hour afterwards, I gave the bark as before; at the next hour he had food, and an hour after that another dose of yeast. He continued to recover, and was soon able to go about his work as usual.

" About a year after this, as I was riding

past a detached farm-house at the outskirts
of the village, I observed the farmer's daughter standing at the door, apparently in great
affliction.   On inquiring into the cause of
her distress, she told me her father was
dying.   I went into the house, and found
him in the last stage of putrid fever.   His
tongue was black, his pulse was scarcely
perceptible, and he lay stretched out like a
corpse, in a state of drowsy insensibility.   I
immediately procured some yeast, which I
diluted with water, and poured it down his
throat.   I then left him, with little hope
of recovery.   I returned to him in about
two hours, and found him sensible and able
to converse.   I then gave him a dose of
bark.   He afterwards took, at proper intervals, some refreshment.   I stayed with him
till he repeated the yeast, and then left him,
with directions how to proceed.   I called

upon him the next morning at nine o'clock, and found him apparently recovered. He was an old man, upwards of seventy."

To these, and similar instances related by Mr. Cartwright himself, might be added several others, confirmed by practitioners of eminence, to whom he had communicated his discovery. The subject having been noticed by Dr. Thornton, in his interesting work on the Philosophy of Medicine, and by Dr. Beddoes, in " Considerations on the Medicinal Use and Production of Factitious Airs," as well as by other medical writers, it is unnecessary to enlarge upon it in this place, or to trace the connexion between the principle of Mr. Cartwright's experiment and the modern practice of administering medicine in a state of effervescence in putrid complaints. The discovery might, in some measure, be called an accidental one; but it was one of those accidents of which men of quick and intelligent minds only, in whom the habit of observation is constantly on the alert, know how to avail themselves.

Mr. Cartwright having been presented to the living of Goadby Marwood, in Leicestershire, he removed thither with his family in 1779. Here he employed part of his leisure time in cultivating his little glebe, and in this occupation appears to have yielded freely to the peculiar bent of his inquiring mind; for his whole system of farming was little else than a series of experiments. But his experiments were not ruinous, and this may be considered as having been the most happy, as it undoubtedly was the most tranquil, portion of his life.

He was at this period a contributor to the Monthly Review, and Mr. Griffiths, the respectable editor of that publication, was a

much-esteemed friend.   When Dr. Johnson
pronounced the writers for that work to be
dull men who *read* their books, he must be
allowed to have passed no small eulogium
upon them ; and indeed, from the whole
tenour of Mr. Griffiths' confidential correspondence with Mr. Cartwright, it appeared
to have been his earnest desire that the
work should be conducted with candour and
integrity, and be, what it professed to be, a
review of the literary productions of the
day, and not merely a medium for the diffusion of party principles.   Even Dr. Johnson,
although in his celebrated interview with
George III. he scrupled not to represent the
Monthly reviewers as enemies to the church
and all establishments, was compelled to do
justice to their care and impartiality.   The
worthy editor seems to have been duly
watchful of the *motives* that might be supposed to influence any of the writers en-

gaged in the work; and though his scrupulous honesty might impose some restraint on
the indulgence of personal feeling as well as
of party spirit, yet was the loss of enter-
tainment that might ensue from such restraint more than compensated to the reader
by the sound sense and good taste which
sought to direct, and not mislead, his judgment. Mr. Griffiths, alluding, in one of his
letters, to a gentleman who had formerly
belonged to the corps of reviewers, observes,
that " he is a learned and ingenious man,
but I would not trust him when he reviews
the works of a *friend*, nor indeed of an
enemy, for in either case no impartiality is
to be expected from him. Poor Langhorne
was the same, and many a scuffle have we
had about *favour* and *resentment*. Pray,
sir, when are you and I to begin to scuffle?
I see no signs of a rupture yet."

No one could bring a more cool and

unimpassioned temper into the service of
literary criticism than Mr. Cartwright, or
a judgment less liable to be biassed by
political feeling. He was, however, no com-
promiser of the interests of religion and
morality, and has been heard in later years
to express great satisfaction on reflecting
that, amongst other castigations inflicted on
the violation of morals and good taste, he
had especially exposed the fallacy and dangerous tendency of the opinions contained
in the works of certain German writers,
then becoming popular. A review of " An
American Farmer's Letters, by Hector
St. John," was one of the articles in the
" Monthly Review" that are now known to
have been from Mr. Cartwright's pen.
These letters were published by Mr. Thomas
Davies,* who, in a letter to Mr. Griffiths,

* See Johnson's Life.

says—" I can ascertain their authenticity, for I am acquainted with the author. He is a man of plain and simple manners, with a strong and enlightened understanding. You will perceive that he has not argumentatively touched upon the great question which unhappily divided us from our North American colonies. His feelings upon the apprehended expulsion from his farm, which really took place, are expressed with such force and energy as cannot be feigned. He who wrote the chapter of the distresses of a frontier farmer must have felt them, or he could not so naturally have described them." It appears that Dr. Johnson's " Lives of the Poets" were reviewed by Mr. Cartwright; and Mr. Griffiths, in a letter relative to that publication, enters at large upon a subject, now indeed of little moment, but which seemed then to have been interesting to literary men—viz., the share that Theophilus Cibber really had had in the compilation of certain lives of the poets that were published in his name.

MR. GRIFFITHS TO MR. CARTWRIGHT.

" Turnham Green, June 16th.

" DEAR SIR,—I have sent you a FEAST! Johnson's *new* volumes of the ' Lives of the Poets.' You will observe that Savage's life is one of the volumes. I suppose it is the same which he published about thirty years ago, and therefore you will not be obliged to notice it otherwise than in the course of enumeration. In the account of Hammond, my good friend Samuel has stumbled on a material circumstance in the publication of Cibber's Lives of the Poets. He intimates that Cibber never saw the work. This is a reflection on the bookseller, your humble servant. The bookseller has now in his possession Theophilus Cibber's receipt for twenty guineas, (Johnson says ten,) in consideration of which he engaged to ' revise, correct, and improve, the work, and also to affix his name in the title-page. Mr. Cibber did accordingly very punctually revise every sheet; he made numerous corrections, and added many improvements—particularly in those lives which came down to his own times, and brought him within the circle of his own and his father's literary acquaintance, especially in the dramatic line. To the best of my recollection he gave *some* entire lives, besides inserting abundance of paragraphs, of notes, anecdotes, and remarks, in those which were compiled by Shiells and other writers. I say *other*, because many of the best pieces of biography in that collection were not written by Shiells, but by superior hands. In short, the engagement of Cibber, or some other *Englishman*, to superintend what Shiells in particular should offer, was a measure absolutely necessary, not only to guard against his Scotticisms, and other defects of expression, but his virulent Jacobitism, which inclined him to abuse every Whig character that came in his way. This, indeed, he would have done, but Cibber (a staunch Williamite) opposed and prevented him, insomuch that a violent quarrel arose on the subject. By the way, it seems to me, that Shiells' Jacobitism has been the only circumstance that has procured him the regard of Mr. Johnson, and the favourable mention that he has made (in the paragraph referred to) of Shiells' ' virtuous Life and pious End'— expressions that must draw a smile from every one who knows, as I did, the real character of Robert Shiells. And now, what think you of noticing this matter, in regard to truth and the fair fame of the honest bookseller!"*

MR. GRIFFITHS TO MR. CARTWRIGHT.

"July, 1780.

" I send you the Candidate, an epistle to the Monthly Reviewers, which, on account of the peculiar compliment to *us*, may de-

---

* Boswell, in his " Life of Dr. Johnson," having recorded a conversation in which the latter expressed his belief that Shiells was the sole compiler of the work in question, a correction of this statement appeared in the " Monthly Review" for May, 1792, and which Mr. Boswell candidly inserted in a subsequent edition of his work. The statement there corresponds exactly with Griffiths' confidential account of the matter; and the editor of Johnson's Life candidly adds, " this explanation appears to me very satisfactory."

serve particular attention. You will doubtless find—

> 'As a friend,
> Something to blame, and something to commend.'

Perhaps you will think with me that this
poem will particularly call for criticism,—
generous and manly criticism, as well as
liberal praise where due; but at all events
it must not be thought that we are to be
coaxed out of our judgment; if this were
the case we should soon have plenty of such
compliments. I cannot guess at the writer
of this Candidate for literary fame."

This poem is now known to have been
one of the earliest publications of Mr. Crabbe,
and though it must be considered as falling far short of the excellence of his later
productions, it appears to have excited no
inconsiderable degree of attention and curi-

osity on the part of those to whom it was addressed. In a subsequent letter, Mr. Griffiths observes—" As the Candidate is addressed to the *corps*, perhaps you may like to hear something of the general opinion of your learned associates concerning it. What I have collected is as follows: ' that although we may not be able to speak so well of the poem as the author wishes us to do, yet it must be allowed that he possesses talents; and many lines are exceedingly good, and much in the manner of Pope, while others are flat and prosaic; that his ardour ought not to be discouraged; that the capital fault of the piece is, that it wants a subject to make a proper and forcible impression on the mind.' On the whole, I cannot help thinking that this Candidate merits encouragement; and yet I dare say you will agree with me that the merit of his poem is not great enough for extraordinary praise." The reception that the Candidate met with from the Reviewers, happily was not such as to repress the poetic spirit of its gifted author; and if this little poem possessed no other merit, it would be highly interesting as a sketch, however slight and imperfect, from the hand of so great a master. His own peculiar style may be traced in it along with those touches, sometimes of self-confidence, sometimes of timidity, which not unfrequently exist together in a powerful, yet susceptible mind. Notwithstanding the intimacy that afterwards subsisted between the author of the Candidate and his reviewer, there is no reason to think that they were known to each other as such. Mr. Cartwright subsequently became one of Mr. Crabbe's warmest admirers.

One more extract from the correspondence of honest Griffiths may be permitted, as affording a useful admonition to the biographer, who, conscious how few passages in a *real* life are calculated to *amuse* the generality of readers, may be tempted to supply the deficiency by filling up his pages with insignificant or gossiping details. "We agree likewise in opinion as to the compilement of *****'s Memoirs, which are, indeed, put together in a slovenly manner; but my greatest objection lies in the *minutiæ* with which those two great volumes are *bumped out*, as the printers phrase it. Had all the *frivolous*, and, I may add, *old womanish* things which are inserted been left out, the book would have been less tedious, as well as less expensive."

The retired habits of Mr. Cartwright's life, as well as the profession of which he was a member, had hitherto kept him from taking any active part in politics, although his opinions were pretty much in unison with those of his brother, Major Cartwright, who already began to be well known as the advocate of parliamentary reform. In 1780, Mr., afterwards Sir William Jones, was proposed as a candidate to represent the university of Oxford; and, on this occasion, Mr. Cartwright made him a voluntary offer of his vote, explaining his reasons for so doing in the following letter to a friend and connexion of his family, who had applied for his interest in favour of another candidate:—

"DEAR SIR,—I have this moment received a letter from Lady Tyrconnel,* intimating that you were much interested in

* Elizabeth, relict of John, Viscount Tyrconnel, and sister to Mr. Cartwright's father.

the success of Sir William Dolben, at the approaching election for the University of Oxford, and that you are desirous that I should embrace the same sentiments with yourself. Unfortunately it is not in my power, much as I may wish to pay attention to your recommendation, to comply with your request. Immediately when I heard that Mr. Jones, (a character for whom I have always expressed the highest esteem and veneration,) was a candidate, I voluntarily made him an offer of my vote, and I wrote also to my old tutor, Mr. Coulson, of University College, who applied to me in favour of Dr. Scott, that as far as the doctor's interest interfered not with Mr. Jones's, he should have the preference to every one else who might be proposed. My motive for espousing these gentlemen rather than any other competitors, was founded not

only on the opinion I had formed of their
integrity, which it would be criminal to
overlook, but I must own also in the interest I felt in the dignity and reputation of
the University. A society, principally instituted for the cultivation of letters, and
which is supposed at least to consist of literary men, cannot, it is presumed, be so re-
spectably, or indeed so properly represented,
as by men who are most conspicuous for
literary attainments; and it seems but just
that those whose superior abilities and learning reflect honour upon the University,
should have in return such honours conferred upon them as the University may
have it in their power to bestow. Upon
these principles, it will be no reflection upon
any man to be postponed to such men as Mr.
Jones and Dr. Scott. I can assure you it is
a matter of considerable mortification to me,
impressed as I am with the remembrance of

your repeated kindness, and desirous of expressing my sense of it on every occasion that shall offer itself, that in the present instance I am prevented giving that kind of testimony which seems to be required from me of the respect with which I am, dear Sir, &c.

"EDMUND CARTWRIGHT.

"Goadby, May 30, 1780."

Until the departure of Sir William Jones for India, in the spring of 1783, Mr. Cartwright enjoyed the gratification of an intimacy and correspondence with that highly gifted man, whose untimely death was considered by him as a private affliction, as well as a public misfortune. Several of Sir William Jones's letters to Dr. Cartwright have been published in his life by Lord Teignmouth.* The following, which is dated

* See Teignmouth's Memoirs of Sir W. Jones, p. 216, *et seq.*

from the Temple, 24th March, 1783, may not be unacceptable to the reader:—

" Allow me, dear Sir, so far to disobey you as to acknowledge the receipt of two very obliging letters, and to thank you most cordially for the friendly expressions which they contain. I am, indeed, much hurried, partly by serious business, partly by troublesome though necessary forms, and have no time to write the thousandth part of what I could say if I had the happiness of being with you. I have no thoughts at present of collecting my political or literary tracts, but am equally flattered by your obliging offer. There is a press at Malda, and another at Calcutta, where I hope to print some eastern varieties; and if I can bring the Persian epic poem to Europe in an English dress, I shall be as far below Lycurgus as Firdusi is below Homer, but shall think the analogy just, and my country will be obliged to me. The family in Hampshire, to whom I read your sweet poems at Christmas, heard them with delight. I am, dear Sir, your much obliged, and ever faithful

" WILLIAM JONES."

During Mr. Cartwright's residence in the Vale of Belvoir, the circle of his intimates became enriched by the addition of one whose works contain, perhaps, the most inexhaustible source of interest of all the productions of that bright constellation of British poets which has illumined the close of the last, and beginning of the present century. About the year 1783, the Rev. George Crabbe became a near neighbour to Mr. Cartwright, and subsequently a valued friend. Although in after life they happened to be much separated, they still kept up a correspondence by letter for nearly

forty years, and most interesting is it to
contemplate in the correspondence of Mr.
Crabbe a mind unchanged through all the
vicissitudes of life, and retaining the same
unaffected simplicity when arrived at eminence, that had adorned it in obscurity and
retirement. He had already published, with
his name, " The Village," and " The
Library," both of which poems had met with
the approbation of Dr. Johnson, Mr. Burke,
and other literary judges of the day. The
time had not then arrived for the public in
general to appreciate justly the promise
which these poems held out of still better
things, and Mr. Cartwright has been often
heard to express his surprise that they had
not received more notice, as well as his regret that Mr. Crabbe did not exercise his
powerful genius on some more extended
work. He had subsequently the gratifica-

tion of seeing the public, as it were, awakened to a due sense of his friend's extraordinary merit.   Twenty-five years afterwards, Mr. Crabbe published a new edition of his earlier pieces, with the addition of the "Parish Register," a poem in which his graphic pen has given the deepest interest to the humblest scenes, by the mere power of faithful delineation; and which can hardly fail to be read with undiminished delight as long as any sympathy with truth and nature, any perception of genuine pathos, shall exist.*

As his subsequent poems are so well known, and have been so justly admired, it may not be uninteresting (though some-

* The editor of this little Memoir cannot forbear expressing the high gratification derived from perusing the interesting Life of Mr. Crabbe, published by his son in 1834.

D

what anticipating the order of time) to introduce in this place an amusing description, given by Mr. Crabbe, of the notoriety they had brought upon him.

FROM MR. CRABBE TO DR. CARTWRIGHT.

"June, 1813.

" Now, my dear sir, I begin to think that I am, as it were, a great man!—a man to be spoken of — not so much as Nicholson, who killed his master, or Peg Nicholson, who would have killed his Majesty, but still spoken of, in an honest way, enough to have it called fame ; for, look ye, I have letters addressed to me, as an author, from strangers and strange admirers, and is not that fame ? Oh ! that Hatchard's current were as flattering. No less than four letters from gentlemen and ladies lie at this time before me; and I

make my boast of them to you, as I intended to do to Sir Walter Scott, whose
letter of the 18th I have to reply to, and
I will let him know what a man I am. A
gentleman from town insists that I have
my picture painted, and prints taken for
my books. Again, a lady invites me (she
knows not my age, nor I hers) into the
mountainous countries, that I may witness
the sublime of nature, and describe it in
that beautiful†   *   *   *   *
Well, thirdly, another lady offers me a
narrative for a new work, which, if related
in my pathetic†   *   *   *   *
and lastly, I have a young poet's request
for an opinion of his verses, mixed, you
may be sure, with notable things said of
my own."

† These blanks are in the original letter.

The selections that have been made from the correspondence of Dr. Cartwright's early friends, are introduced chiefly for the purpose of shewing that there was nothing in the pursuits of the first half of his life calculated to lead his mind to study the theory of mechanics, or in his habits to bring him acquainted with their practical application. His pursuits had been purely literary, and his associates were as unknowing as himself in everything relating to manufactures. He was not only esteemed for the elegance of his attainments, but he had also at that time a fair prospect of advancement in his profession, and of attaining a competency sufficient for the liberal support of his station in society. A circumstance, altogether accidental, now occurred to occasion an entire change in all his views, and to turn his mind into a different direction, from which it never afterwards diverged, but continued, even as life advanced, to pursue its object with undiminished intenseness.

CHAPTER II.

In the summer of 1784, Mr. Cartwright happening to be at Matlock, in Derbyshire, became, during his visit there, highly interested in the progress of those ingenious manufactures, which not many years before had been established in that immediate neighbourhood. The application of machinery to the art of spinning was at that time a novelty; and the splendid fortunes that some ingenious mechanics, who had been successful in introducing it, were

supposed to be realizing,* seemed to hold
out extraordinary encouragement to the exercise of any inventive faculty that should
contribute to the improvement of our national manufactures. Mr. Cartwright was
not aware in how high a degree a faculty
of this nature existed in his own mind,
until it was brought into action by the
accidental occurrence of a conversation at
the public table, on the subject of new and
ingenious inventions, especially that of Sir
Richard Arkwright's recently invented method of spinning cotton by machinery.

It was observed by some of the company
present, that if this new mode of spinning

---

* In proof of the extent to which these expectations were subsequently fulfilled, we may here refer
to the fact, that Mr. Arkwright, (son of Sir Richard),
who is just deceased, is stated to have left behind
him a fortune of not less than *seven millions* sterling.

by machinery should be generally adopted, so much more yarn would be manufactured than our own weavers could work up, that the consequence would be a considerable export to the Continent, where it might be woven into cloth so cheaply, as to injure the trade in England.* Mr. Cartwright replied to this observation, that the only remedy for such an evil would be to apply the power of machinery to the art of weaving as well as to that of spinning, by contriving looms to work up the yarn as fast as it was produced by the spindle. Some gentlemen from Manchester, who

* The fulfilment of this prediction, twenty years subsequently to the above conversation, in fact led to the first adoption of the power-loom, which came afterwards into more general use, from the great demand for English cotton goods, in consequence of the disturbed state of the Continent.

were present, and who, it may be presumed, were better acquainted with the subject of discussion, would not admit of the possibility of such a contrivance, on account of the variety of movements required in the operation of weaving. Mr. Cartwright, who, if he ever had seen weaving by hand, had certainly paid no particular attention to the process by which it was performed, maintained that there was no real impossibility in applying power to any part of the most complicated machine, (producing as an instance the automaton chess-player,) and that whatever variety of movements the art of weaving might require, he did not doubt but that the skilful application of mechanism might produce them. The discussion having proceeded to some length, it made so strong an impression on Mr. Cartwright's mind, that immediately on his return home, he set about endeavouring to construct a machine that should justify the proposition he had advanced, of the practicability of weaving by machinery. It may be remarked, that the incredulity expressed by those gentlemen, who were of all persons most likely to be acquainted with the fact, had any attempt been previously made to weave by machinery, is a pretty decisive proof that nothing of the kind had then been effected.

His first attempts, as might be supposed, were rude and clumsy ; but as neither drawings nor models now remain of them, we have no means of tracing his earliest steps in mechanical experiment, nor of ascertaining the mode in which he proposed to overcome difficulties that had appeared insurmountable even to experienced mechanicians.

In the course of a few months, however, he had brought his loom to such a state of progress, as led him to imagine that it might eventually become profitable; and to the surprise of every one who was at all conversant with undertakings of this nature, as well as to that of his personal friends, he took out a patent in April, 1785, in order to secure to himself the expected advantages of the invention.

The patent, or, as it is now called, the power-loom, has doubtless been receiving continual additions from various hands during the last fifty years; and the beautiful machine (adapted as it is to every variety of fabric, and now in use to an immense extent) differs considerably in detail, even from the most improved form of Mr. Cartwright's invention. But to him the merit is due of having been the first to apply power successfully to the business of weaving, and the principles by which he achieved that first great step, may be traced through every progressive improvement; and unquestionably opened the way to many of those ingenious additions by means of which later mechanists have brought the power-loom to its present state of excellence. Before we proceed further in relating the progress of Mr. Cartwright's mechanical career, it may be necessary to give a slight sketch of the mode in which hand-weaving is usually performed; in order that the reader who is not conversant with such subjects, may be enabled to form a clear idea of the nature of the movements required, and to produce which, manual dexterity was considered indispensable.

The annexed plate represents the principal features of a common hand-loom, consist-

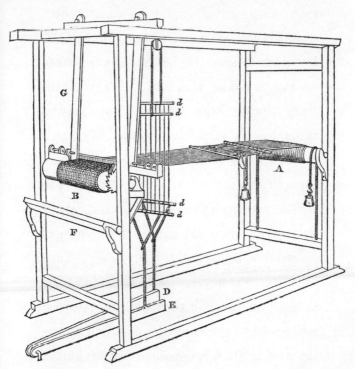

ing of, *A*, the yarn beam; *B*, cloth beam;
DE, treadles; *dd*, heddles [or healds];
G, lay or lathe, including the reed; *F*, seat
board.

In the operation of weaving, the workman being seated on the board F, moves with his feet alternately the treadles DE, by which motion the heddles are depressed or raised. The alternate threads of the warp having been separated by passing through each respective heddle, the action of the heddle produces the shed, or space through which the shuttle has to pass. The shuttle is thrown from hand to hand, whilst the weaver with the hand last disengaged throws the lay or lathe back in an oblique direction, which being suspended from the upper frame-work of the loom, and returned to its natural perpendicular position, presses the woof or thread, deposited by the shuttle, close to the cloth already woven.

In this operation, the alternate action up and down of the heddles, the alternate action transversely of the shuttle, with the additional one of throwing back the lathe, have all to be produced by the hands and feet of the workman, without the aid of any intermediate instrument, that might have suggested to the mind of a novice in mechanics a feasible method of applying machinery to the purpose. The fly-shuttle might indeed be considered as an approximation towards a more improved practice; but that ingenious contrivance, although invented by Mr. Kay as early as the year 1738, does not appear to have been in general use when Mr. Cartwright first gave his attention to the subject.

Mr. Cartwright's first power-loom, as described in the specification of 1785, was, as may be supposed, a somewhat rude contrivance, and differed materially from the form which he afterwards gave to it. The warp was placed perpendicularly, and the shuttle was thrown by springs connected with a cylinder placed beneath the machine. This cylinder also gave motion to two levers, one of which reversed the threads of the warp, and the other elevated the reed, which again descended by means of its own weight. The tension of the warp was produced by weights suspended from the beams, as in the common loom.

This simple apparatus rapidly received great modifications from Mr. Cartwright's hands, as is shewn in his several specifications of 1786, 1787, and 1790. The warp was now placed horizontally, and the several parts of the machine were adjusted in a form which in its general features scarcely differs from the power-loom of the present day. The application of a crank on the axis of a wheel communicating with the moving power, was the mode by which Mr. Cartwright effected the alternate motion of the lathe. Simple and obvious as such a contrivance may now seem to those who are in the habit of seeing hundreds of power-looms in daily operation, yet before his time it does not appear to have been thought of; and in this invention alone he may be considered as having made no small progress towards weaving by machinery. It is probable that a contrivance for throwing the shuttle, so as to make it pass and repass, and yet keep within its prescribed bounds, did not so readily occur to his mind; for the compiler of this memoir has a perfect recollection of the amusement it used to afford his children to watch their father, imitating the action of a weaver throwing his shuttle, as he walked up and down the room absorbed in his new speculations.

He succeeded, however, in overcoming this difficulty, by means of tappets fixed on the axis of a wheel communicating with the moving power.*   These tappets give action to the treadles, which being connected by means of strings with the picker,† (an apparatus placed at each end of the box in which the shuttle moves,) an impulse is thereby communicated to the picker, which causes it to throw the shuttle from side to side with an accuracy superior to that of the hand.   In like manner was the requisite action of the heddles or healds produced, and those three principal actions being thus accomplished, the foundation was laid for

* A tappet is a wheel, or portion of a wheel, fixed eccentrically upon an axis.   The treadle being kept in contact with the tappet, is alternately raised and depressed as the lathe revolves.

† In the North of England, to *pick*, means to throw; and therefore the name of picker is applied by the workmen to express that part of the machine which throws the fly-shuttle.

those manifold improvements which have progressively been made in the application of mechanical power to weaving, and of which Mr. Cartwright's invention still forms the leading principle.

The reader will find in the Appendix a figure and description of a portion of Mr. Cartwright's power-loom, as modified by him in 1790, including a method for stopping the loom on the breaking of the thread, which is very similar to that still in use. Further improvements were afterwards introduced by him, and secured by patent in 1792; among which are a plan for weaving checks by means of a double shuttle-box— for tightening the selvage—and for making the lathe give a sharp blow. The limits of this work do not admit of our entering into greater detail respecting these less important features of Mr. Cartwright's mechanical labours.

That he had early imparted to some of his friends the hopes he began to entertain of the success of his new invention, will appear from the letters of Mr. Crabbe, to whom he communicated from time to time the progress of his mechanical labours. In December, 1784, within very few months of Mr. Cartwright's first attempt at weaving, his friend the poet writes—" You shall not find me smiling at your loom when you grow serious in it. I have the worst mechanical conception that any man can have, but you have my best wishes. May you weave your webs of gold!"

"Belvoir Castle, Feb. 14, 1785.

" I am not a little surprised at what you tell me of your enterprise. I have a thousand good wishes for your success, without one idea of your contrivance. Mrs. Crabbe has a better conception of your plan, and no less desire that you may accomplish it. I am about my contrivances too, but mine is spinning—spinning flimsy verses. Dodsley shall manufacture them, and send you a sample."

"Belvoir Castle, May, 1785.

"Fortune smile upon your undertaking; or, not to be heathenish on a serious subject, God bless you in it,—only remember when you grow very rich, that we were friends before, and do not look down on us as the summer birds that will then come and serenade you daily. They talk here of your machine, but they are shy of us; if they say any other than well, it is amongst themselves, and I scarcely meet with anybody who has any opinion at all upon the subject."

Although the actual production of his loom was of a humbler texture than that anticipated in the kind wishes of his friend, yet Mr. Cartwright considered it sufficiently satisfactory to induce him to present a specimen of it to Mrs. Crabbe; for, in June, 1785, Mr. Crabbe says, " I have just time to thank you for your letter, and to present my wife's thanks for your cloth, of which she is very proud. I need not repeat my congratulations, nor our wishes. I, who never· had a mechanical idea in my life, begin to lament my want of capacity to comprehend, in some measure, how these things can be; but I comfort myself that my ignorance is not, as ignorance generally is, of the malignant kind."

In 1785, some property in the town and neighbourhood of Doncaster having devolved to Mr. Cartwright and his family, he was induced to fix his residence principally in that place, where finding skilful workmen more attainable than in a country village, he applied himself with increasing energy to the perfecting of a contrivance in which he had already made no inconsiderable progress. Early in the year 1786, he visited Manchester, partly with the view of engaging some of the superior workmen of that place to assist him in the construction of a more perfect model of his machine than he had hitherto been able to accomplish, and also in the hope that some of the opulent and enterprising manufacturers of that flourishing town might be induced to enter into his views, and give effect to the productions of his inventive genius, by the aid of their practical knowledge. The following letter to his friend, the Rev. W. U. Wray, contains a description of his early difficulties, as well as of his subsequent expectations of success :—

" When I arrived at this place (Manchester) I found my machine not even begun upon; indeed, the workmen who had undertaken it, despaired of ever making it answer the purpose it was intended for, and therefore, I suppose, were not willing to consume their time upon a fruitless pursuit. I have, however, the pleasure to tell you, that the whole system of it is now finally adjusted, and so much so, both to mine and the workmen's conviction, that we cannot entertain the shadow of a doubt respecting its success. I have taken some pains to make myself acquainted with the manufactures of this place, which has much contributed to the perfection of what I have been aiming at. I cannot forbear telling you, that the machine is so exceedingly simple and cheap, as not to cost (after the model is once made to work) above five or six pounds."

By another letter to the same gentleman,

written also from Manchester, in May, 1786, the fact is ascertained of his having at that time effected an improvement in his loom, which was subsequently considered of great importance—viz., the stopping of itself of the machine, on the accidental breaking of a thread : " Respecting my business, sorry am I to say that it seems very little nearer a conclusion than when you left me. Delay upon delay. It is a satisfaction, however, that the delay does not arise from any unforeseen difficulty. The apparatus for stopping when the thread breaks, either in the warp or woof, is completed, and performs its business with the greatest accuracy and facility." A projector may overrate his own success, or an experimentalist be disappointed even in the best founded expectations; and, therefore, the ill fortune that pursued Mr. Cartwright for so many years

E

of his life might be considered as the not
unusual lot of the ingenious; but it was
much more remarkable, that he should live
to see his self-confidence completely justified.
Twenty years afterwards, from the very
place where the machine that he describes
first struggled into existence, and where it
was most especially decried and opposed, a
memorial from several of the most influential
manufacturers was offered to the legislature,
in which it was stated that Mr. Cartwright's
looms were employed there to the extent of
several thousands.

During his temporary residence at Manchester he continued to report the progress
of his experiments to Mr. Crabbe, who expresses his participation in his success in the
following pleasant terms:—

"May 8th, 1786.

" Every new hope you give me of your success makes me happy, and I believe you cannot have more zealous well wishers for it than Mrs. Crabbe and myself, nor am I disinterested, since I expect to be maintained handsomely as a decayed poet, and my wife is scheming every day to entitle herself to a pension for decayed projectors."

"May 27th, 1786.

"I am rejoiced to hear so happy an account of your prospects. I do not think the time long that you take for the completion of your labours, in any respect, but that of your being absent. You wrong your mechanical talent, for though chance might help you at first, it must be a chance indeed that could carry you on so without skill. You only mean, I conclude, that you know mechanics practically, without having a mathematical foundation to build upon; nor had Archimedes himself, that we know of, I believe."

The little encouragement that Mr. Cartwright met with at the time from persons already engaged in manufacturing concerns, was probably the cause of his deciding on a somewhat hazardous undertaking; no less than the establishment, under his own direction, of a weaving and spinning factory at Doncaster, and in which free scope might be given to every description of mechanical experiment. Having engaged the most skilful workmen he could procure, he continued to make repeated alterations in his loom; and one branch of mechanism leading to another, he effected important improvements in the art of spinning as well as in that of weaving.

The capability of the weaving-machine seemed now to be unequivocally proved. From the report of an aged person now living, who was employed at the factory at its first commencement, it appears that twenty looms were shortly set to work; ten for muslin, or muslinette, eight for cotton, one for sail-cloth, and one for coloured check. The machinery was at first worked by a bull, but in 1788 or 1789, he set up a steam-engine.

It may be presumed that the fabric produced in this infant manufactory was of some excellence, from the following letter from Mr. Cartwright's old friend, Dr. Thurlow, Bishop of Durham, to whose lady he had presented a piece of muslin:—

" DEAR SIR,—I am ashamed, when I look at the date of your letter, to have so long neglected to acknowledge the pleasure Mrs. Thurlow and I received from its contents. We were exceedingly glad to find that you have so happily and fully succeeded in all your machinery, and no less happy to hear that it is likely to prove so very lucrative to the ingenious mechanic. We most sincerely hope that it will prove as productive of advantage as of renown to the inventor, and that he and the public will be equally benefited by his various and ingenious contrivances.

"Mrs. Thurlow, who has been for some weeks confined, is at last come abroad, and has determined to put herself into a dress made out of the piece of muslinette you were so good as to present her, and which for its novelty, and being the first fruits of your labours and art, she prizes beyond the richest productions of the East.

" We hope to see you in Doncaster as we pass through to London, and then and there will you receive my wife's thanks for your kind and, in many respects, valuable present, and our united congratulations on your success. At present, I conceive, you are so much taken up with your machinations (for they must not be denominated manufactures), that we must not entertain a hope of seeing you at Auckland before the Christmas holidays, soon after which we propose leaving this part of the world. If you can find leisure and inclination to take such a journey, no one can be more glad to see you (for as long a visit as you can make) than, my dear sir, your affectionate humble servant,

" THOS. DURESME.

" Auckland, Oct. 24th, 1787."

It is probable that a piece of muslin even such as the lady of a bishop would not disdain to wear in 1787, would, under any circumstances, be of a quality very inferior to what is now produced; but that inferiority would proceed no less from the spinning than the weaving. Notwithstanding the wonderful inventions of Hargreaves, Arkwright, and Crompton, &c., the art of cotton-spinning might be said to be in its infancy, compared with the perfection to which it has since been brought. The finest yarn then produced would hardly have made a piece of •muslin such as a lady now would think fit to wear.

However gratifying to Dr. Cartwright's feelings the progress of his new discoveries might be, it soon became evident that the establishment at Doncaster, on the whole, was far from being profitable. The " factory system" was then in its infancy, and his own want of experience in the details of business such as he was now engaged in, occasioned all the work under his direction to be done at a more than ordinary expense. And being in some cases dependent on other branches of manufacture for the completion of his own, he was continually exposed to the influence of a narrow-minded jealousy, which now began to operate against him, but which probably proceeded from a growing conviction, on the part of the manufacturing interest, of the importance of his invention.* Various petty means were practised, in order to obstruct the popula-

* " The same spirit of opposition that Mr. C. met with had driven Mr. Kay, the inventor of the fly-shuttle, from England, as well as Hargreaves, the inventor of the spinning-jenny, from his native place, to settle in Nottingham; but a more striking

rity of the machine-woven goods. The
cottons sent by Mr. Cartwright to be printed
were frequently rendered unsaleable, by
obsolete patterns and imperfect execution;
and of his best and most uninjured articles,
the chief consumption was in presents to his
friends, or in supplying furniture for his own
house. In the meantime, the extraordinary
ingenuity of the invention itself, as well as
the peculiar circumstances under which it
first appeared, had awakened a considerable
degree of interest, and Mr. Cartwright, as
might have been expected, was by turns
admired for the vigour of his inventive
genius, and condemned for the rashness of
his speculations. Attempts also were made

instance of prejudice, was the opposition to Sir
Richard Arkwright's application for relief from a
duty on calico."—*See* Baines' Hist. of Cotton
Manufacture.

to seduce his workmen, as well as to evade his patent right, by using his machine differently modified; and, indeed, the openness with which he frequently communicated his ideas, joined to the extreme easiness of his temper, rendered such attempts at piracy by no means difficult, and tended eventually to involve him in several vexatious disputes and expensive lawsuits.

He had not taken into the account, that ingenuity alone was not sufficient to ensure protection, for a man of his character and habits, in the path he had newly entered on; and when he ventured to emulate the successful enterprise of others, he did not consider that its most striking examples were in men who had either risen from the working, or still belonged to the manufacturing classes. Neither did he calculate on the importance of being trained to habits of

industry and business, or on the necessity of
a far more intimate knowledge than he possessed of the feelings and prejudices of the
class of persons he had to deal with; who
though shrewd and intelligent in their own
immediate line of business, had no very
enlarged views beyond it.

Nor was Mr. Cartwright's new position
in society altogether without its trials. By
the upper class of the inhabitants of a provincial town, proud of their exemption from
commerce and manufactures, his proceedings
were viewed with no small degree of distrust;
and so portentous an innovation as the
introduction of a steam-engine, was received
with expressions of general dissatisfaction.
Although some few of his personal connections and friends participated in his own
sanguine views, and even joined in the
pecuniary part of the speculation, by others

he was considered as having deserted his *caste*, whilst by the more rigid he was condemned for engaging so deeply in occupations unsuited to his profession. With the poor of the place, however, his establishment was far from being equally unpopular. It afforded employment to numbers, without interfering with their previous occupations; and in addition to remuneration for their industry, they were certain of assistance, when required, from his benevolence. His name is still venerated by the descendants of his ancient workmen. To men of ingenuity and talents his house was always open, and in an intelligent and intellectual, though somewhat miscellaneous society, he consoled himself for the reserve of his more fastidious acquaintance. In reverting to this period of Mr. Cartwright's life, we are fully sensible of the change that the last fifty years have produced in the opinions of nearly every class of the community. A man of genius now, whose inventions should tend to increase that general diffusion of the conveniences of life, which marks a truly civilized people, would have more to fear from competition than from prejudice. But at the time when he first commenced his mechanical career, there was a considerable class of persons, who, dreading the advance of every degree in society below themselves, deprecated the progress of machinery, as being the means of supplying the poor with indulgences heretofore confined to the rich, and consequently tending to raise them higher in the scale of refinement than was compatible with the due subordination of society.

It is hardly necessary to combat objections which few persons now will be found to entertain; nor does it come within the object of this volume to discuss so extensive a question as the general results of machinery. But it may be observed that it is the higher classes who have been the greatest gainers by the progress of improvement in the mechanic arts. The elegances and conveniences administered through the practical science of the manufacturer have contributed to raise them from a state of feudal barbarism, in which, from the want of comforts endured by all classes alike, the actual difference of condition between the high and the low, as to many of the appliances of life, was much less decided than it is at present. At a time when the floors of the hall or castle were strewn with rushes, and when the great Earl of Northumberland considered one clean table-cloth per month a sufficient allowance for his upper servants' table, the accommodations of the cottage could hardly have been more homely. And though the lady of rank, when jolting in her cumbrous coach without springs, might display more dignity, she certainly could not enjoy more ease than if she had been travelling in one of her tenant's carts. In the words of the *Quarterly Review*, " the want of every kind of comfort within their houses leaves us nothing to envy of the enjoyments of our forefathers in those good old times, which are the sad burthen of many ' an idle song,' and the constant theme of repining patriots." And when it is considered, on the other hand, how favourable to the health and habits of cleanliness amongst the poor is the cheapness, resulting from machinery, of various articles of clothing, the increase of machinery cannot on the whole be regarded as an evil. It is, indeed, true that recent investigations have disclosed a fearful state of society in some of our manufacturing districts, but we need only look at the factories of Lowell, in the United States, to be convinced that demoralization is not a necessary accompaniment of the Factory System. Had our own manufacturers been less exclusively devoted to the accumulation of wealth, and had the British Government exerted itself sooner to secure to the manufacturing population the advantages of education and of restricted hours of labour, we might have escaped much of the evil which is often, but unjustly, attributed to the progress of mechanical improvements.

In 1786, Mr. Cartwright printed a new edition of his poems. The following letter from his old friend Mr. Griffiths, seems to have concluded the literary correspondence that had subsisted between them for several years. But though from this period their correspondence ceased, their mutual regard remained undiminished:—

" MY DEAR SIR,—I am very much obliged to you for the favour of your letter of the 8th instant, and for the further favour of six copies of your book, three of which shall be immediately disposed of according to your directions; another I propose to give to Wm. Seward, Esq., F.R.S., a very ingenious, good man. I rejoice that you have given me this proof of your not having yet forgotten your old friend—a friend who will always remember and love you.

" Your mill is now, I hope, at work, and working with success. It is kind of you to invite me to see it, which I hope to do in August, after the publication of our appendix, the said appendix always occasioning me a month of slavery in July—by doing double, and more than double duty. Notwithstanding the opinion preconceived by even the best mechanics, I cannot help feeling some apprehensions with regard to the *good going* of the mill, and therefore I shall be solicitous for an early account of its actual performance. By this time, I suppose, a fair trial hath been made, and I shall be very much obliged to you for the news of the result. Sincerely hoping that the success hath been, or is likely to be, fully answerable to your expectations,

" I remain, dear Sir,

" Your truly affectionate, humble servant,

" R. GRIFFITHS.

" Turnham Green, May 22nd, 1787.

" Mrs. G. presents her very respectful compliments, as doth my son George. I hope your brother, the worthy major, is well; I do not forget that I have been obliged to him."

As early as the year 1786, some ideas relative to an improvement in the steam-engine had suggested themselves to Mr. Cartwright's mind; and though it was not until several years later that he took out any patent for a steam-engine, the following letter to a friend is introduced, as marking the period when he first attended to the subject, as well as illustrating his own scrupulous delicacy with regard to the invasion of other men's inventions:—

"DEAR SIR,—I am infinitely obliged to you for your attention in procuring me admission to the Albion mill. You will be surprised when I tell you that I have at present an insuperable objection either to seeing Bolton's steam-engine, or the still more powerful one invented by Sadler of Oxford, which is now in town, and which he has promised to shew me. My reason is, that I am now making a model of one that I have invented myself. I wish to avoid temptation either to borrow or steal. The idea visited me a morning or two ago, as I was under the hands of the hairdresser. I immediately communicated it to some philosophical friends, particularly my neighbour, Mr. Gregory; none of them had the least doubt of its practicability. From the short conversation I had with Sadler, his improvement consists principally in having a double cylinder, so that the steam is condensed both above and below the piston. My *improvement* consists in having neither cylinder, piston, condenser, nor beam; nor, in short, any species of *mechanism*. When my model is finished, which will be in a day or two, you shall hear more of it. I shall leave town in a few days; my next residence, for one week, will be at Goadby, and then at Doncaster.

"I am, dear Sir, most truly yours,

"EDMUND CARTWRIGHT.

"67, Pall Mall, June 10th, 1786."

Whether the model alluded to was completed, or what were the motives for suspending at that time the prosecution of this experiment, cannot now be ascertained. Mr. Cartwright's first patent relative to the steam-engine was taken out in 1797, of which a description will be given hereafter.

CHAPTER III.

MR. CARTWRIGHT, though he had accomplished one great object of his wishes, in contriving
a loom that should be worked by machinery,
was not disposed to stop short in a career
that seemed to him so promising of success.
His next invention, a machine for combing
long wool, may be considered as even more
original than the former.   In the instance
of the loom, he had a machine prepared to
his hands, that was already capable, in one
way, of performing the work required of it,

and the merit of his discovery consisted in applying a new power, in order to produce, to a much greater extent, motion that had hitherto been only produced by hand. But between the very simple act of combing wool by hand and the process of combing it by means of a complicated machine, that should perform the work of *twenty* men, there seemed to have been no intermediate gradation, no introduction, as it were, to a more improved method, by any addition to the instrument in common use, and which is as inartificial as it might have been in the days of Bishop Blaize.*

It is not precisely known when Mr. Cartwright first attempted a machine for combing wool. His earliest patent relative to that invention is dated 22nd August,

---

* A bishop of Sebaste, in Asia Minor, in the third century, and the patron saint of wool-combers.

1789. The contrivance therein specified is altogether different from that of his later machine, and consisted of a cylinder armed with rows of teeth, which is made to revolve in such a manner as that its teeth may catch and clear out the wool contained in the teeth of the fixed and upright comb. But this imperfect method was, not long afterwards, superseded by the contrivance of a circular horizontal comb-table, for which a patent was obtained 27th April, 1790. In this apparatus the teeth of the horizontal table are set vertically, but with a slight inclination towards the centre, and are supplied with wool by means of a circular lasher. Motion is communicated to the different parts of the machine in a very ingenious manner; but the complicated nature of the circular lasher appears liable to objection, and renders it far inferior in effect, as well as in simplicity, to the subsequent contrivance of the *crank-lasher*. For this eminent improvement Mr. Cartwright took out another patent, bearing date 11th December, 1790, including also an alteration in the teeth of the comb-table, which are here set horizontally, and pointing towards the centre. This patent also contains the description of a simple and ingenious apparatus for washing the wool, previously to its being combed.

His fourth patent, which is believed to contain his final improvements relative to this branch of manufacture, is dated 25th May, 1792.

Without entering into a minute detail of the various parts that compose the combing-machine, a short explanation of its leading principles may enable the reader, with the assistance of the annexed plate, to form a

To face page 99.

DR. CARTWRIGHT'S "BIG BEN," OR WOOL-COMBING MACHINE.

clear idea of the mode in which the work is performed. It must first be observed that the wool undergoes a slight preparation by means of a machine called the Preparer, which, though more simple in its construction, as it acts nearly on. the same principles as the finishing machine, need not be described.

The finishing machine consists of an horizontal circular frame A, or comb-table, of perhaps five or six feet diameter, set with teeth pointing to its own centre. In order to feed or fill this circular table, and at the same time to give the wool the first combing, the machine is furnished with a member or limb, called the crank-lasher, B, the action of which, from the number and construction of its joints, is somewhat analogous to the action of the human hand and arm, when the woolcomber in the common mode of operation lashes his wool on a comb fixed in the wall.

At the lower extremity of the crank-lasher are a pair of feeding rollers, C, which draw the wool from a tube with which the lower branch of the lasher is furnished, and regulate the delivery, whilst the lasher lashes it into the principal comb. The wool being thus deposited, undergoes a further operation or clearing, by means of a smaller circular comb, D, which has a revolving motion (produced by a pair of cranks) in a plane at right angles, or nearly so, to the plane of the principal comb, so as that once in every revolution it strikes through the wool of that comb, and clearing it out, leaves it in a fit state to be drawn off by the delivering rollers, E. These rollers are so placed, that by the revolving motion of the principal comb the wool with which it is filled is successively brought within their bite, or grasp, and with the additional action of a pair of callender rollers, F, is thus formed into a long and continuous sliver.

Thus the principal members of the combing-machine, as delineated in the plate, are, A, the circular comb-table; BB, the crank-lashers; CC, the feeding-rollers; D, the clearing-comb; EE, the delivering-rollers; FF, the callender-rollers.

The manner in which power is here applied and communicated, so as to produce at the same time not only several motions, but motions of a totally different character, is strikingly ingenious; and this machine, including its subordinate parts and accompaniments, which in this explanation are omitted, may fairly be accounted one of the most beautiful, as it is, unquestionably, one of the most original, instances of mechanical contrivance.* The inventor having possessed only a slight knowledge of mechanical principles, and yet attaining, within a very short period of time, so extensive a mastery over their application, this instance of his ingenuity is the more remarkable.

How far the principles suggested by Mr. Cartwright in this particular branch of manufacture have since been applied, might, by diligent inquiry, be ascertained; but the features of the original invention, rather than its present applicability, form the object which we have chiefly in view. For more than fifty years the utmost ingenuity of man has been at work to make the most

* A beautiful model of this machine, belonging to Dr. Cartwright's grandson, George Cartwright, Esq., may be seen in the Adelaide Gallery of Art and Science, where it is deposited for the gratification of the curious.

of every previous suggestion, and in new modifications and fresh improvements the original source is frequently lost sight of. Yet although the inventor's name had been forgotten, Mr. Cartwright's loom was known for many years at Manchester by the name of the " Doncaster patent loom ;" and even at the present day the machine used at Leeds for combing wool, is called " Big Ben," the name originally applied to Mr. Cartwright's machine by his workmen at Doncaster.

In the space of seven years he had accomplished two inventions, which promised to lead to most extensive effects on the commerce and manufactures of this country. He had taken out no fewer than nine patents within that period, and these not only for improvements in the two principal arts of weaving and wool-combing, but also including improvements in spinning, callendering linens, cutting of velvet pile, as well as an entirely original machine for making ropes.*

Mr. Cartwright having thus completed his machine for combing wool, the novelty and ingenuity of the contrivance attracted the attention of men of science and distinction, as well as of persons connected with the manufacturing classes. Several of the latter began now to consider this invention, from its prodigious saving of labour, likely to become no less advantageous than that of the loom; and notwithstanding the vast expenses he had incurred in taking out patents both in England and Scotland, and above all, in bringing his machinery to perfection, there now seemed every rational prospect of ample remuneration, from the acknowledged excellence of the inventions. Such, indeed, was the encouragement he

* See Appendix (D).

had met with from those who were supposed
to be best acquainted with the state of our
manufactures at that time, that several of
his friends and immediate connexions were
induced to enter into speculations, of which
his new discoveries were to form the basis.*

Full of hope and expectation, Mr. Cartwright continued to prosecute his mechanical
experiments; and although he became frequently annoyed by attempts to pirate his

* At this period of hope and exultation Mr.
Cartwright indulged himself in giving an entertain-
ment to his workmen. They amused themselves
with a procession, in honour of Bishop Blaize, the
tutelary patron of wool-combers ; and on this occasion, Matthew Charlton, one of the workmen of the
factory, composed a song, which being set to music
by Dr. Millar, became for several years a favourite
and popular air among the lower classes in the
town and neighbourhood of Doncaster.   It is necessary to mention, that the combing-machine obtained
the name of " Big Ben," a noted boxer of the day,

inventions, he considered such attempts as acknowledgments of their importance, and trusted that long before the expiration of his patent rights, his own claim to originality would be sufficiently established to secure the reward which he might reasonably expect from them.

from the action of the crank·lasher, which was thought to resemble the strokes of the pugilist ·—

SONG.—NEW BISHOP BLAIZE.

I.

Come all ye master combers, and hear of new Big Ben,
He'll comb more wool in one day than fifty of your
men,
With their hand-combs and comb·pots, and such old-
fashion'd ways ;
There'll be no more occasion for old Bishop Blaize.

II.

Big Ben was made at Doncaster, that place of great
renown,
And is a noble fellow, supported by the Crown:
Whenever you shall see him he'll put you in amaze,
And make you praise the inventor, our new Bishop
Blaize.

Towards the latter end of the year 1791, a favourable prospect opened for the introduction of his loom into the cotton manufacture of Manchester. Messrs. Grimshaws, of that place, had contracted with Mr. Cartwright for the use of four hundred of his looms, and built a mill calculated to

III.

Our triumph then this day there's nothing shall prevent,
For know, our great mechanic by Providence was sent
For the good of mankind, boys—a trophy, then, we'll raise
To our British Archimedes, our new Bishop Blaize.

IV.

The hungry he gives bread to ; the naked, too, he clothes ;
May health and joy and riches, attend him as he goes:
Then fill your glasses high, boys! and give him three huzzas;
Here's our good and worthy master—our new Bishop Blaize!

receive and work that number. Very soon after the building was completed, and when about four-and-twenty of the looms were set to work, the whole of the edifice was burnt to the ground; and from the threatening letters that had been received by the owners, and other indications of hostility shewn towards this novel establishment, no doubt was entertained at the time of its having been intentionally destroyed.

For reasons best known to the parties most nearly concerned, the circumstances attending the destruction of this mill were not very diligently inquired into. The object of the perpetrators unquestionably was effected—no other manufacturer ventured on repeating so hazardous an experiment, and the consequences to Mr. Cartwright were ruinous.

His contract with Messrs. Grimshaws of

course became void, and as the hostility manifested towards his weaving would in all probability extend to his combing-machine, it seemed hopeless for him any further to prosecute his works at Doncaster, which, for the reasons already stated, had been carried on rather for the purpose of proving the merit of his inventions, than from any hope of profit or advantage arising from the goods there manufactured.

Mr. Cartwright's resources from his own private fortune were beginning to be exhausted, and the severe check now given to his hopes and prospects brought upon him, as might be expected, demands which it required the utmost of his available means to satisfy. After an ineffectual struggle to contend with the tide of prejudice that was now turned against the adoption of his machinery, and to meet the difficulties that were accumulating upon him, Mr. Cartwright found himself obliged to relinquish his works at Doncaster. In the latter part of the year 1793, he assigned over his patent rights to his brothers, John and Charles Cartwright, Esquires, in consequence of the share they had taken in the concern, and as being in circumstances better able to contest the infringements to which, in spite of the outcry raised against them, his inventions were continually subject.

That Mr. Cartwright felt, and deeply felt, the disappointment of his expectations, cannot reasonably be doubted; but it was much less for himself than on account of others, whom his influence and example had encouraged to enter into concerns for which their previous habits and education rendered them wholly unfit, but who might not equally be able to follow his example in fortitude.

With the self-confidence of conscious ability, he still believed that time would prove what he was himself convinced of—the value of his inventions,—and so far from entertaining any feelings of envy towards those more successful introducers of new machinery, who were already realizing splendid fortunes, his sanguine spirit, deriving only encouragement from their example, abated nothing of its elasticity and vigour.

The following sonnet was composed by Mr. Cartwright, at the close of this disastrous year:—

SONNET.

With sails expanding to the gales of hope,
  My venturous bark pursued her leading star;
Hers was a voyage of no common scope,
  A voyage of Discovery, distant far!
To bright INVENTION's intellectual clime,
  In search of USEFUL ARTS, 'twas mine to roam.
I reach'd the object of my views sublime,
  And richly freighted, bore my cargo home.

My friends expectant fill the crowded strand;

   But ere I gain the shore, what storms arise!

My vessel founders e'en in sight of land!

   And now a wreck upon the beach she lies!

With firm, unshaken mind that wreck I see,

     " Nor think the doom of man should be reversed

       for me."

CHAPTER IV.

It might perhaps have been expected that Mr. Cartwright, after he had experienced so discouraging a check in his mechanical career, would naturally have returned to that peaceful mode of life, and those literary pursuits, in which he had passed the best and happiest of his years; but it was now too late to retrace his steps and relinquish a path still attractive, though beset with difficulties. He had, indeed, missed the sources of worldly wealth, but he had opened on so rich a vein, in his own mind, of new and ingenious perceptions, conducive, apparently, to the benefit of his fellow-creatures, that benevolence and philanthropy came in aid to sanction the indulgence of his inclination, and in continuing to pursue his mechanical discoveries, he judged that he might not unworthily employ the talent he was entrusted with.

In the summer of 1796, Mr. Cartwright removed with his family* to London, as being a situation more favourable than a distant provincial town, for the cultivation of scientific pursuits. He rented a small house in Marylebone Fields, of Mr. James Wyatt, the late celebrated architect, who had given considerable encouragement to a

---

* His first wife died in 1785, and in 1790 he married Susannah, the youngest daughter of the Rev. Dr. Kearney.

new invention by Mr. Cartwright, for which he had taken out a patent the preceding year. This was for an improvement in the form of bricks, by means of which, an arch might be supported on a wall of the usual thickness, and consequently might be employed with advantage in many cases where the thickness of the support required to sustain an arch built in the common method is an objection to its use. In order to ascertain the efficiency of this invention, an arched room was built with these geometrical bricks, in addition to the house Mr. Cartwright occupied. The height of the arch is not now remembered, but being somewhat flat, it gave no unpleasing appearance to the apartment, which was used as a dining-room. An untoward circumstance occurred in the outset of this experiment, that would have discouraged most men from proceeding further; but Mr. Cartwright never seemed to lose sight of Lord Bacon's consolatory reflection, "that no man ought to be discouraged if the experiments he puts in practice answer not his expectation, for what succeeds pleaseth more, but what succeeds not, many times informs no less." Owing to the negligence of the workmen, in removing the centres before the work was dry, and an error in the construction of the wall, in no way referable to the principle of the invention, the first trial had failed, but the building being resumed, with the advantage of experience, the plan was found completely to answer, and Mr. Cartwright continued to reside in the house to which the addition above described was made, until October, 1801. When the Regent's Park was laid out, some years afterwards, it became necessary to pull down the house in question, which stood very nearly on the site of the present Coliseum. The building was found to be so exceedingly compact and strong, that it required more than ordinary labour to destroy it.

As this invention was well known to architects and engineers, engaged in works for which, to all appearance, it was peculiarly calculated, and as the most eminent amongst them did not at that time point out any probable objection to its use, it seems extraordinary that in no instance, as far as is known, save in the solitary one above recorded, (and in which its entire success had been unequivocally proved,) has it been adopted; even where strength and security from fire were objects of such paramount importance as to render the mere difference of expense between the patent and the common bricks a matter of very inferior consideration.

In the " Repertory of Arts," edited by W. H. Wyatt, vol. iii. p. 84, will be found a full description of the geometrical bricks. " It is obvious that arches on this principle, having no lateral pressure, can neither expand at the foot, nor spring at the crown, therefore they will want no abutments, requiring only perpendicular walls to rest on; and they will want no incumbent weight to prevent their springing up—a circumstance of great importance in building bridges. Their greatest advantage is security against fire."*

The expense of making the geometrical bricks, in consequence of the precision they require, may seem an objection to their use for common purposes. From a drawing found amongst Mr. Cartwright's papers, he appears to have had a plan for making them

* These bricks are described in the Appendix (E).

by machinery, which would greatly have
facilitated their construction, and contributed to their exactness; and now that such
rapid advances are daily making in the
application of power, it is not too much to
expect (since the principle of the invention
seems unobjectionable) that a means may
be discovered of removing the only objection
to the use of these bricks, by lessening the
expense of making them.

In October, 1797, Mr. Cartwright took
out a patent " for an incombustible substitute for certain materials commonly used in
constructing dwelling-houses." The invention consisted in applying tiles made of fire-
clay, instead of laths, reeds, or boards, in
making ceilings, partitions, and floors. The
tiles were made long enough to reach from
centre to centre of the spars or joists, to
which they were fastened by nails or cramps

driven through notches made in each end of the tiles, the joints being closed by mortar or cement. For floors, no further process was required; but for walls and ceilings a coat of plaster was added, which it was proposed to render more adhesive by means of grooves on the surface of the tiles.

It does not appear to what extent this very simple invention was adopted in practice, but there can be no doubt that a plan is here suggested, the general use of which would greatly diminish the frequency of those dreadful conflagrations which render a residence in large towns perilous both to property and life.

Another of his inventions, about the same period, is described in the second volume of the "Repertory of Arts." It is a method for applying the treadwheel to the working of cranes. There can be no doubt, that in all cases where it is requisite to produce a rotatory action by human labour, the tread-wheel presents the simplest and most effectual means of applying the power. The muscles of the lower extremities being in the human subject much more strongly developed than those of the arms and thorax, it is evident that a machine worked by means of the legs must have much greater power than the common winch-handle, which is worked by the upper portion of the body only. More-over, the action of *walking* being one for which the human frame is especially adapted, the application of this action to mechanical purposes is far less likely to be injurious to the health than any more constrained and artificial motion. In the plan before us, the treadwheel communicates the motion to the windlass of the crane, not by cogs, but by a worm or screw upon its own axis, which

G

obviates all risk of the wheel running back, in consequence of the weight overcoming the power of the man who works it. At the other end of the axis of the treadwheel is a winch, and the weight having been raised, the treadwheel is disconnected by means of a coupling-box, and the weight is then lowered by turning the winch in an opposite direction.

It has been already stated that Mr. Cartwright had entertained some ideas relative to improvements in the steam-engine, as early as the year 1786. But it is not known whether the scheme he then formed was ever attempted in practice. His first patent for a steam-engine was obtained in 1797.

A description of this engine, accompanied with a beautiful engraving, forms the first number of that excellent work, the " Philosophical Magazine," edited by the late Mr. Tilloch, and first published in June, 1798; and a further account of this invention is introduced in the "Descriptive History of the Steam-engine," by Mr. Stewart, who bears a most liberal testimony to its ingenuity. An extract from the former of these works will explain the principles upon which Mr. Cartwright proposed to remedy the defects to which the most improved engine was subject. "These defects, as every one knows, are an imperfect vacuum, much friction, and complicated construction of parts; liable, without great care and attention, to be frequently out of order. It is to these points Mr. Cartwright has immediately, and we may add, successfully, directed his attention. His first object seems to have been to obtain, as nearly as may be, an absolute vacuum; which, in consequence of the elas-

tic vapour that separates from water injected
in the usual mode of condensation, no one in
the least conversant with the philosophy of
the steam-engine need be told is impossible.
The condensation in his engine is performed
by the application of cold to the external
surface of the vessel containing the steam.
Mr. Cartwright is not, however, the first
who tried this method; the same has been
attempted by several, but with so little success, that one of our first engineers in this
line has been heard to give it as his opinion,
that were a pipe to be laid across the
Thames, the condensation would not be
quick enough to work a steam-engine with
its full effect. The manner in which Mr.
Cartwright manages this business is by admitting the steam between two metal cylinders, lying one within the other, and having
cold water flowing through the inner one,

and inclosing the outer one. By these means a very thin body of steam is exposed to the greatest possible surface. But this is not all;—by means of a valve in the piston there is a constant communication at all times between the condenser and the cylinder, either above or below the piston, so that, whether it ascends or descends, the condensation is always taking place.

To reduce the friction of the piston, which, when fresh packed in the common way, lays a very heavy load upon the engine, Mr. Cartwright makes his solely of metal, and expansive. There is a further advantage in this method, from the saving of time and expense in the packing, and from the piston fixing more accurately, if possible, the more it is worked.

Mr. Cartwright has been equally attentive in simplifying all the other parts of the engine—his engine having only two valves; and those are as nearly self-acting as may be.

But what will probably be esteemed one of the most important circumstances attending these improvements, is the opportunity they afford of substituting ardent spirit, either wholly or in part, in the place of water, for working the engine. For as the fluid with which it is worked is made to circulate through the engine without mixture or diminution, the using alcohol, after the first supply, can be attended with little or no expense; on the contrary, the advantage will be great, probably equal to the saving of half the fuel. When, indeed, the engine is applied, as Mr. Cartwright occasionally purposes, both as a mechanical power and as a still at the same time, the whole fuel will be saved. A further advantage of this invention is its applicability to purposes requiring only a small power, and for which any other engine would be too complicated and expensive."—See "Phil. Mag.," June, 1798. Mr. Stewart observes, that the details of this engine " are constructed with uncommon ingenuity, and that the whole apparatus may be considered more simple and efficient than any other combination which had been proposed of the parts of the condensing engine." He concludes a very clear and interesting explanation of its construction, by further observing, " that the machine, from its refined simplicity, appears excellently adapted as a first mover on a small scale. It has never, however, had a fair trial. The objections which were urged against the condensing vessels, at the time of the invention, have always appeared to us more specious than solid. To the great merit in the arrangement and simplification of parts shewn in this engine, must be added one of immense importance to engines on every construction—the *metallic piston*. Mr. Cartwright constructed his of two plates, between which were placed detached pieces of metal; instead of the usual packing, these pieces were acted upon by a spring, so as always to be kept equally tight, whatever might be the wear of the piston. The manner of connecting the piston-rod and procuring a rotatory motion is a beautiful specimen of mechanical invention."— *Stewart*, p. 157.

The following references to the plate, representing a section of the steam-engine, will enable the reader to understand the method by which the condensation is performed, as well as the extraordinarily ingenious contrivance of the metallic piston, with its springs. *A*, the cylinder; *B*, the piston; *I*, the pipe which conducts the steam to C, the condenser, being a double cylinder, between which the steam passes into the pump D, that serves for returning the condensed fluid back into the boiler; E, the air-box, with its valve.

The pipe from the pump, through which the condensed fluid is returned into the boiler, passes through the air-box. The air, or elastic vapour, that may be mixed with the fluid, rises in the box till the ball which keeps the valve shut falls, and suffers it to escape.

F, the steam-valve; G, the piston-valve. When the piston B reaches the bottom of the cylinder A, the tail or spindle of the valve G being pressed upwards, opens the valve and forms a communication between the upper side of the piston and the condenser; at the same moment the valve F is pressed into its seat by the descent of the

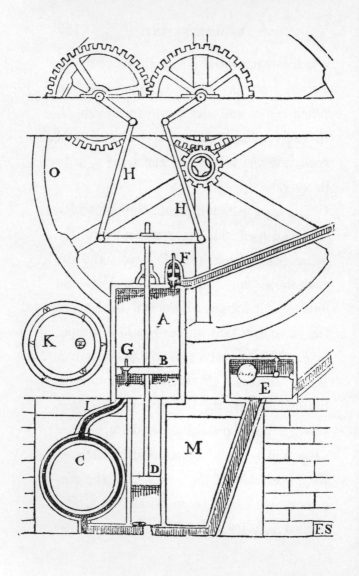

cross-arm on the piston, which prevents the further admission of steam from the boiler, thus allowing the piston to be drawn up to the top of the cylinder by the momentum of the fly-wheel O; $H H$, two cranks, upon whose axles are two equal wheels working in each other, for the purpose of giving a rectilinear direction to the piston-rod; M, the box that contains the condensed water.

K, plan of the piston, shewing the metal rings, which by the springs are forced outwardly against the inside of the cylinder, so that the piston can adapt itself to any inequality that may arise.

In the same patent that Mr. Cartwright obtained for the above engine he also proposed a modification of the rotatory engine, described by Mr. Watt in 1782. See " Repertory of Arts," vol. x. p. 7.

By his removal to the metropolis, Mr.

Cartwright enlarged the sphere of his acquaintance amongst men of ingenuity and science; and his house again became the resort of projectors of various merits and pretensions. His own manners were peculiarly calculated to make his society coveted where his talents were admired. No man who knew so much was so little pertinacious in conversation; he had a thorough contempt for arrogance; and though satire was a weapon he could occasionally wield with no small effect, he was conscientiously forbearing in the use of it: but the quality that of all others recommended him to that description of persons who principally sought his society, was his remarkable openness, and freedom from jealousy towards rival and contemporary projectors.

Amongst other ingenious characters who frequented Mr. Cartwright's house, may be

noticed one who was then deeply engaged
in pursuits similar to his own, but whose
claims to originality of invention have not
been very willingly admitted on this side of
the Atlantic.   This person was Robert Fulton, well known in America as being the
first engineer who navigated a steam-boat
in that country, and not altogether unknown
in Europe for his experiments in submarine
navigation.   He was a native of New Jersey, in the United States, and had come to
England with the intention of studying
painting under his countryman, West.
Having abandoned painting as a profession,
he applied himself to civil engineering, and
in that line of business had been noticed by
Earl Stanhope, with whom he had had communication on the *practicability of moving
vessels by steam*, as early as the year 1796.
At this time, also, navigating by steam was

one of Mr. Cartwright's favourite projects, and he conceived that his newly invented steam-engine might be made applicable to that purpose. It may appear superfluous, where so much originality of invention can be substantiated, to allude to any claims that may be considered doubtful; it is, however, well known that Mr. Cartwright did construct the model of a boat, which being wound up like a clock, moved on the water, so as to prove the experiment in a manner satisfactory to the inventor; though, as this little model was afterwards given away as a toy, and has long been destroyed, there are no means of ascertaining how the machinery was adjusted, or what resemblance it might bear to the method since adopted in the working of steam-boats.

The coincidence of their respective views, produced, instead of rivalship, intimacy and friendship between the two projectors, and Mr. Fulton's vivacity of character and original way of thinking rendered him a welcome guest at Mr. Cartwright's house. The practicability of steam navigation, with the most feasible mode of effecting it, became a frequent subject of discourse. The writer of these memoirs has now to regret, amongst many other neglected opportunities of acquiring knowledge, that, from the carelessness of youth, such a degree of attention was not given at the time to these discussions as might have thrown considerable light upon a subject, since become of such universal interest. Who could then contemplate, when Mr. Fulton was drawing the plans of his paddle-wheels, and Mr. Cartwright contriving how his steam-engine should act upon them, that speculations apparently so chimerical should have been realized to their present wonderful extent! It is not assumed that Mr. Fulton, even with Mr. Cartwright's assistance, had at that time brought his plan of a steam-boat to any great degree of maturity; but it is believed that neither of these gentlemen were then aware of any other person having advanced towards steam navigation as far as themselves. Nor will this appear improbable, when it is considered that it was then a mere project, a chimera entertained only by a few projectors, who might be carrying on their respective schemes in distant parts of the kingdom, without any knowledge of each other's contrivances, although in aiming at the same project, and through the same means, they might hit upon the same mode of applying those means. An instance of this kind of coincidence is alluded to by Mr. Fulton, in his Treatise on Canal Navigation, in which he candidly acknowledges having been anticipated in a contrivance that he had conceived to be original; but a more striking instance of a revived invention, possessing all the merit of originality, is that of Mr. Watt, who cannot be said to owe the great improvement that rendered his steam-engine so eminently applicable to the purposes of machinery, to Mr. Jonathan Hulls, although Mr. Hulls had suggested the same idea many years before.* If a

* " Although Mr. Jonathan Hulls did not originate any novelty in the construction of the atmospheric engine, he is entitled to the honourable notice of having proposed the application of paddle-wheels moved by a steam-engine, to propel ships, instead of wind and sails. In this scheme it was necessary to *convert the alternate rectilineal motion of a piston-rod into a continuous rotatory one,* and which he ingeniously suggested might be accomplished by means of a *crank.* This is now, with justice, considered to

person hit upon an invention that he never
heard of, it is original in him; and if it be
the result of patient study, or a habit of
observation, he may be allowed to be a
meritorious, if not a fortunate inventor;
but if, by his energy and spirit of enterprise,
he succeed in introducing into practice
what others, perhaps, had only contemplated
in theory, he is entitled to additional credit,
without disparaging that of his predecessors.

In 1797, Mr. Fulton went to France, at

be that invention which introduced the steam-engine
as a first mover of *every variety of machinery.*
Hulls was unable to interest the public in his projects; and his mode of applying the crank was so
completely forgotten, that at its revival, about forty
years after this period, a patent was obtained for the
invention, and the merit of the application was also
claimed by the celebrated Mr. Watt, evidently without any knowledge of Hull's suggestion."—*Stewart,
Hist. Steam-Engine,* page 8.

that period under the government of the Directory, and did not return to England until the latter end of 1802, or beginning of 1803, having passed a portion of the intervening time in America. From his correspondence with Mr. Cartwright, such passages may be selected as appear to have reference to those mechanical subjects on which they were both deeply engaged. He writes from Paris, July, 1797:—

" After being detained at Calais three weeks, waiting for a passport, I made a circuit of about three hundred miles; and on arriving at Paris, I found the Directory had given a special order for my passport, which was sent to Calais after my departure; thus there is every symptom of my remaining here in peace, although the Americans are by no means well received or suffered to rest in quiet.

" The country through which I travelled is like a continued field, in excellent cultivation, and all the districts of France are said to be in an equally good state; thus plenty will relieve the burthens of war. *But what do I say of war?* In Paris one would suppose they had never heard of it, for all is gay and joyous. As to business, I cannot yet say much; but I have reason to believe there will be good encouragement to men of genius, and improvement will be rapid on the termination of the war. Please to let me know the state of your ideas relative to the steam-boat, &c.

" R. FULTON."

"Paris, Sept. 20th, 1797.

"MY DEAR SIR,—I have not had an opportunity of answering your letter of the 20th August till now. I am much pleased with

your mode of making houses fire-proof, and
should be happy to see it extended to
America; but I do not think that Mr.
* * * * or * * * * would answer your
purpose; because whoever takes up such
subjects must be active, and have the business at heart. On these points I have mentioned to you, that providing me with
descriptions and powers, I shall be happy to
do my best for you in America; but if you
could sell the invention for a reasonable sum,
I should think it advisable. My idea of
many of those things, which may be considered as only the *overflowings of your
mind*, is to convert them into cash, and
adhere firmly, even without partners, to
some of your more important objects, such
as the steam-engine, boat moving by steam,
or cordelier. I have a great objection to
partners. I never would have but one if I
could help it, and that should be a wife."

"Paris, Nov. 28th, 1797.

" I have received yours of the 12th instant, and am happy to hear of the success of your steam-engine, and other improvements, for the extension of which I will endeavour to make an arrangement when I have the pleasure of seeing you. In this country there are but few engines, and the principal are at the collieries, near Valenciennes. I am well acquainted with the proprietor, who informs me there is little hope of introducing such improvements into France till the termination of the war; but when peace returns, I conceive every encouragement will be given to the arts, and France will rise, like a phœnix, from the ashes of war."

"Paris, Feb. 16th, 1798.

" DEAR SIR,—I have received yours of December 11th, at which time you could not have received my last letter, which was dated December 8th. You speak of expecting my return, but that, I fear, is very doubtful, in consequence of the delays at the patent-office, the approaching period when I must necessarily return to America, and the difficulty of obtaining a passport from hence to England. Should these causes prevent me from again seeing your family, in whose short acquaintance I took much delight, and whose taste for science flattered me with the prospect of much pleasure on my return; yet I hope we shall keep up the acquaintance which the art of writing may preserve; and believe me, I shall ever feel interested in the progress of science or fortune in your family. Hitherto I have been like a wanderer in life—but in America I hope to become reasonably stationary, where, assembling a few friends around me, I may pursue

my plans of public improvement with patient
industry.   Works of magnitude, I find, cannot be hurried.   It would give me much
pleasure to make the produce of your mind
productive to you.   You will, therefore,
consider what part of your inventions I may
be intrusted with.   The steam-engine, I
hope, may be made useful in cutting canals,
and moving boats, so that it will be directly
in my line of business.   By the bye, I have
just proved an experiment on moving boats
with a fly of four parts, similar to that of a
smoke-jack; thus,

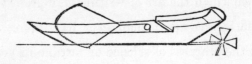

I find this apply the power to great advantage, and it is extremely simple.*   The

* It is very interesting to remark, that in this,
the earliest of Mr. Fulton's schemes for steam navi-

patent law is now altering, but I fear the price will not be reduced, yet the payments will, perhaps, be made easy, by being 20*l.* per year for three years. My small canals are making many friends; which business I shall leave under the guidance of a company. The celebrated Montgolfier has just made a great discovery in hydraulics; it is a means of raising water from the beds of rivers by the simple movement of the stream, without either pump or wheel. I know him well, and have seen his model frequently at work. It is forty feet high, and consisting of only two tubes, extremely simple. I also have been contriving a curious machine for mending the system of politics, and applying

gation, we see the principle of the "Archimedes screw," which, though for many years superseded by the "paddle-wheel," is now likely to come into universal use.

H

manual labour to advantage.   Of these two
inventions I will send you sketches before
my departure.   Believe me, &c.,

"ROBT. FULTON."

"Paris, June 20th, 1798.

"MY DEAR SIR,—Still I continue in
France, and thus take the opportunity of
writing to you by my friend, Mr. Gilpin,
who will convey to America anything you
have to communicate to me on mechanical
subjects.   In a long letter I wrote to you on
mechanics, on March 5th, I mentioned some
ideas of a machine for making ropes, the
model of which is now finished, capable of
making a rope one inch diameter.   By Mr.
G. I send you a piece of rope fabricated on
the engine, by which you may judge of its
state of perfection.   But still I conceive you
have superior ideas on the movement of such

an engine, particularly the means of giving equal tension to all the strands.

" I shall hope for a very particular letter on mechanics when Mr. G. arrives in America, with sketches, if not models, of, 1st, steam-engine; 2nd, steam-boat, 3rd, cordelier, &c. &c."

At this time Mr. Fulton was engaged in prosecuting his experiments in submarine navigation; but that he also pursued his projects of moving boats by steam appears by the following letters to Mr. Cartwright, whose recent invention seemed peculiarly applicable to Mr. Fulton's purpose:—

"Paris, 10th March, 1802.

" MY GOOD FRIEND,—Be so kind as to let me know how you have succeeded in your steam-engine. To what state of perfection

H 2

have you brought it? What will one of a
six-horse power, making a three or four foot
stroke, cost? How much will it weigh?
How much space will it require when rendered as compact as possible? What weight
and value of coals will it consume per hour?
and how soon can it be made? I think you
once mentioned to me your intention to use
spirits of wine, and that you could obtain
a power of at least 30lbs. to the square inch.
Have you succeeded in these great objects?
The object of these inquiries is to make part
of an examination on the possibility of
moving boats of about six or seven tons by
steam-engine, and your engine I conceive
best calculated for such a work; particularly
as the condenser may always have the advantage of cold water without adding much
to the weight of the boat; and having the
advantage of cold water may enable you to

work with ardent spirits, and produce the
desired elasticity of steam with one-half the
heat,—hence, in calculating the weight of
the whole apparatus, the weight of the condensing water will be trifling, it is therefore
the *weight of the engine and the fluid in
the boiler which are to be calculated.* For
this object I believe the engine should be
double, with the steam acting on the top and
bottom of the piston, or in two cylinders, the
one ascending while the other descends.
For the particular case, where such a boat is
wanted, I believe it is of more importance to
have a light and compact engine, than to have
too much regard to the economy of fuel, unless the additional weight of the fuel to go
twenty miles would be more than the additional weight of the engine to economize the
heat. To gain power in a small space, how
would it answer to make the boiler suffi-

ciently strong to heat the steam to two atmospheres, or 30 pounds to the square inch?—thus, a cylinder of six inches would give a purchase of 300 pounds; that is, 900 pounds' constant purchase, which is about the sum of my demand,—as for example, three pounds will draw a piece of timber 20 feet long, which presents a butt-end of one foot square, at the speed of

1 mile per hour.

12 pounds, 2 ditto - ditto.

48   „   4 ditto - ditto.

96   „   6 ditto - ditto.

120   „   7 ditto - ditto.

Now, supposing my boat to be 40 feet long and five feet wide—boat, passengers, and engine, weighing six tons—it will present a front of about six feet resistance, or 720 pounds' purchase, to run such a boat seven miles per hour.

Suppose the boat to weigh . . . . . 2 tons,

30 passengers, with their baggage $\frac{3}{5}$,,

one ton is left for the engine and machinery. From this calculation you will be able to judge what can be done by your invention; and if by your means I can perfect my plan, I have got a good opportunity of rendering your engine productive to you, and it will give me pleasure to do so. You will be so good as write to me as soon as possible, answering, in a particular manner, the questions stated, with any observations you think proper and will be so good as to make on my proposed attempt.

"ROBT. FULTON."

Mr. Cartwright's reply to the above inquiries was, doubtless, given under a strong impression of the value of his invention, and produced the following letter from his sanguine correspondent:—

"Paris, 28th March, 1802.

" MY DEAR SIR,—It is with great pleasure I have received your flattering account of your steam-engine; and although attachment to you makes me believe everything you say, yet such belief is merely a work of faith, for I cannot see the reason why you have 13½ pounds' purchase to the square inch. Is this in consequence of the friction taken off the piston by your circles?* How have you found that mode to answer? Is it that, by your mode of condensing, the water becomes deprived of its air, and that the steam may be heated four, five, or more pounds per inch above the atmosphere? If

* The metallic rings—an invention of acknowledged ingenuity and usefulness. (See page 131, supra.)

the engine can be made so light as you mention, and give only ten pounds to the square inch, it will answer my purpose; but it must be a double engine, making thirty double strokes, or sixty single strokes, per minute, of three feet each; that is to say, three feet per second. As I can afford to give five feet by six for the engine, it will not be necessary to place the cylinder in the boiler. If it stands outside of the boiler, repairs can be made with more ease; but when we have decided on the engine, I will give a sketch of the mode in which I propose it should stand, to give movement to the machinery which is to drive the boat. If, for my case, you propose to condense without injection, the condensing vessel may be a long cylinder or tube, with another tube through its centre, through which a current of water will pass with a velocity equal to

the speed of the boat, and thus carry off the
caloric very quick. I do not see how the
engine, water in the boiler, and fly included,
can weigh so little as a ton, and, say, a half.
What will be the weight and diameter of the
fly? Another important consideration—is
it permitted to send such engines out of the
country? the design is to America. The
smoke-jack flyers will not answer for a quick
movement. Reduced to two arms, thus,

it answers admirably for my plunging-boat,
where the velocity is not more than two
miles per hour, between two waters, and
where oars cannot be used. I was so
pleased with it in that experiment, that I
last summer built a pinish* thirty-six feet
long and five feet wide, extremely light, and

* Commonly written *pinnace*.—ED.

of the best workmanship. I placed in her
quadruple cranks, from bow to stern, thus,

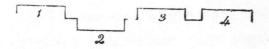

to each of which were six men, total twenty-
four of the best seamen of the fleet. The
multiplication from the crank to the flyers
was at first fourteen to one; the flyers, four
feet diameter; angle, thirty degrees. We
could not make more than four miles per
hour. I reduced the multiplication to
seven for one. We went about four miles,
but with less fatigue to the men. I changed
the diameter of the flyers from four down to
two feet, and the angle from forty down
gradually, five degrees at a time, to fifteen
degrees. Still our speed was never more
than about four miles per hour. When the
boat gains a certain velocity, the water run-

ning quick past the flyers, they lose their purchase; and multiplying them to a velocity so as to overtake the boat, or strike the running water sufficiently quick, causes a friction, which consumes much of the power. However, I have found an excellent mode of taking my purchase on the water in all possible velocities, and where the whole power will be applied to advantage. The question now is only to find the best steam-engine to put it in movement; and I sincerely hope it will be yours. For political reasons, I have never yet confided to *but one person* the combination of my plunging-boat, and committed the whole to drawing and explanations, in case of any accident happening to me; however, it will be satisfactory to you to know that the experiments have been very successful. I was very fortunate in surmounting some great difficulties; and navigating under water is now easy to be performed, and without risk."

In the " Annual Register" for 1802, is an account of Mr. Fulton's diving-boat, taken from the relation of citizen St. Aubin, a man of letters at Paris, and member of the Tribunate, which confirms the inventor's own statement of the success of his experiment. " I have," says Monsieur St. Aubin, "just been to inspect the plan and section of a nautilus, or diving-boat, invented by Mr. Fulton, similar to that with which he lately made his curious and interesting experiment at Havre and Brest. The diving-boat, in the construction of which he is now employed, will be capacious enough to contain eight men, and provision enough for twenty days, and will be of sufficient strength and power to enable him to plunge one hundred feet under water, if necessary. He has constructed a reservoir for air, which will enable eight men to remain under water for eight hours. When the boat is above water, it has two sails, and looks just like a common boat. When she is to dive, the mast and sails are struck. In making his experiment at Havre, Mr. Fulton not only remained a whole hour under water, with three of his companions, but kept his boat parallel to the horizon at any given depth. He proved that the compass points as correctly under water as on the surface; and that, while under water, the boat made way at the rate of half a league an hour, by means constructed for that purpose."—Vol. xliv.

Whatever might be the ingenuity of the contrivance, or merit when effected, of the *bateau plongeur*, it is certain that Earl Stanhope, no incompetent judge of mecha-

nical and scientific subjects, entertained a
formidable idea of its efficiency, and earnestly
endeavoured to impress upon the English
government a sense of the danger that might
arise to this country, in consequence of the
French nation having taken the American,
Mr. Fulton, under their protection.   In the
following year (1803) his lordship again
referred to Mr. Fulton's contrivance for
blowing-up ships under water, and stated in
the House of Lords that he had himself given
a plan to the Admiralty, for preventing the
effect of an invention, which he considered
of so formidable a nature.

It is evident that the art of navigating
under water might convey an awful power
into the hands of any one who possessed it;
and consequently the British ministry did
not think it unworthy of inquiry how far
Mr. Fulton's pretension to success, in so for=

midable an art, was well founded or not.
Mr. Cartwright, who was probably in full
possession of Mr. Fulton's secret, and no less
impressed than Earl Stanhope with the no-
tion of its dangerous extent, was consulted
in this inquiry.　On the renewal of the war,
Mr. Fulton's neutrality, at least, was considered worth the purchase; and Mr. Cartwright was appointed one of the arbitrators
to settle the terms upon which Mr. Fulton
consented to the suppression of his secret.
The terms of the award were probably satisfactory to Mr. Fulton.　He returned to
America not long after the arrangement
alluded to, and in the following summer
(1807) he had the satisfaction of seeing
accomplished his long-cherished and favourite project of launching a steam-boat in his
native country.　As Mr. Fulton's name is
introduced into this memoir solely with a

reference to his intimacy with Mr. Cartwright, it is not necessary to enter more at length into the question of the extent to which he might, or might not, have availed himself of the inventions of others. It is certain that he owed much to his own ingenuity for the success that attended his first experiment at New York; and still more to that activity of mind and spirit of enterprise, which enabled him so to establish steam navigation in America, that its obvious advantages there should have led to its extended adoption, not only in this country, but in every part of the civilized world.

This ingenious and enterprising man died at New York, in the year 1815, in the forty-ninth year of his age.

CHAPTER V.

In November, 1798, Mr. Cartwright became a member of the " Society for the Encouragement of Arts, Manufactures, &c. ;" and in October of the following year, he was recommended by his friends to offer himself as a candidate for the situation of secretary to the society, recently become vacant by the death of Mr. Samuel Moore. The candidate being on this occasion required to present a memorial of his pretensions, Mr. Cartwright, on the 18th December, read

before the society an address, from which
the following extracts are taken:—

" The qualifications more particularly
looked for in the person who is to fill the
important office of secretary to this society,
are, I understand, practical knowledge and
experience in those matters which are its
leading objects.   These are, chemistry, the
polite arts, agriculture, manufactures, and
mechanics.   It is expected, also, that he
should know something of the modern languages.   The only living languages I ever
was acquainted with, are the French and
Italian, and though disuse for a long series
of years has nearly obliterated them from
my recollection, I do not feel, however, as if
I should have much difficulty in recovering
them, and, in the meantime, I should take
care that the society should experience no
inconvenience on that account.   Of che-

mistry, though I am not ignorant of its elementary principles, my knowledge is much too limited to speak of it with any degree of confidence. In this department, therefore, I am free to confess you will not find my acquirements of that service to you I could wish, and yet I flatter myself you will not find them altogether useless. That they have not been altogether useless to the world, I need only appeal to that most invaluable discovery—the method of administering, in the form of yeast, the carbonic acid gas; a discovery which, not only in this island, but in various parts of the globe, has already, in innumerable instances, proved an inestimable benefit to the human race. You will perceive I am alluding to the almost invariable success with which this remedy has been administered in cases of putrid fever, and as a specific in that cruel disease,

the sea scurvy. Those only who have experienced that sublimest of enjoyments, the
pleasure of benefiting mankind, can appreciate the satisfaction I have had in its discovery."

" But of all the objects which engage the
attention of this society, the principal, and,
without dispute, the most important, is
agriculture; an art which, at the present
awful period, more, perhaps, than at any
former one, requires the exertions of every
enlightened mind to bring it to its highest
stage of practical perfection. That much is
to be done, it is unnecessary to observe, for
till such time as every field shall be a garden, agriculture has certainly not arrived at
its acme. That this is no ideal point of
improvement to look forward to, we need
only advert to the state of this art amongst
the Chinese, and the manner in which they

are at once compelled and enabled to prac-
tise it by an overflowing population. With
us, the great mass of population being
diverted into other channels, other means
are to be resorted to. The combined ener-
gies of various arts must be employed;
chemistry must lend her inexhaustible
stores—mechanics, her hundred arms. The
one, by calling into action the latent
principles of nature, gives to vegetation
renewed life and increase of fertility; the
other, by furnishing man with multiplied
ability, giving to a pigmy the powers of a
giant. But no combination of science in
agriculture will avail without practical
knowledge; and in no art, so indispensable
as this, is practical knowledge required from
your secretary. On every other subject,
information or assistance, in a city like this,
may be met with in every street, and at

every hour ; for here is the resort of genius
and talents in every department of science,
not only because they are here most encouraged, but because they are here also most
conveniently cultivated.   With agriculture
and its professors it is otherwise.   Agriculture is not to be practised in cities, nor has
a city life allurements for a mind devoted
to its pursuits.   On this subject, therefore,
more frequently than on any other, must
your secretary depend on the stores and
resources of his own mind.   These stores
are not to be collected from books or theory,
nor from the speculative opinions of artists,
mechanics, chemists, or philosophers; they
must be the result of real practice and repeated observation, under different circumstances, and at different seasons.   On this
ground I feel to tread with confidence ; for
during nearly thirty years of my past life

my constant residence has been in the country, and for a considerable part of that time
those hours which were not occupied by the
duties of my profession, or devoted to literary pursuits, were chiefly employed in the
practice and study of agriculture. I may
truly affirm there are few experiments in
that most useful and interesting pursuit
which I have not either tried myself, or
witnessed the trial of by others.

" Respecting manufactures and practical
mechanics, it will be no boast in me to say,
—what, indeed, so many here present can
probably confirm,—that few men have had
greater experience than myself; still fewer,
I should hope, have purchased that experience at so dear a rate.   The manufactures
I am most immediately acquainted with, are
those extensive ones of cotton and wool;
every process of which I am acquainted

with, from the raw state of the article till perfected in the loom.

" There are several other manufactures, also, of which you will not find me ignorant.

" That I may not detain you too long by reciting all the different mechanical inventions of magnitude and importance that I have at various times brought forward, I shall enumerate only three; and these three, as you will perceive, are in departments of invention totally distinct from each other. These are, the method of combing wool by machinery; the geometrical principle of constructing arches, so as to have no lateral pressure; and the late improvements I have made in the steam-engine. By that single invention of combing wool by machinery, the manufacturers are at this moment saving at least 40,000*l.* a year, and in a short space of time will annually save between

I

one and two millions. By the geometrical principle of constructing arches, so as to have no lateral pressure, buildings may be erected at as little expense as they now are, and be perfectly secure from fire. And by my improvement on the steam-engine, I have so added to its power, and reduced its expense, that it may not only be employed in manufactures more extensively than it has hitherto been, but may be made also a most powerful and profitable agent in husbandry, as will, I hope, be exhibited on an extensive scale in the course of next summer.

" There are many other circumstances in a long, and, I may say, useful life of unwearied exertion, which might, with propriety, have been brought forward; but I have confined myself to those chiefly which, being of public notoriety, the public, if anything has been stated unfairly, has the means of confuting.

" Permit me to trespass on your time one moment longer. Since the death of Mr. Moore, a very unusual number of new members, I am told, has been admitted into the society; many, it is possible, for the mere purpose of voting at the ensuing election. There are, I trust, no friends of mine who have gained admittance from any such motive. If they have, I must request they will either not vote at all, or bestow their votes on some other candidate. For myself, I should feel it a disgrace to owe that to private interference which it would be my ambition to obtain by the public voice. If I am to succeed I will succeed only by fair and honourable competition."

This memorial was received with so much favour by the society, that little doubt was entertained of Mr. Cartwright's success, had he been inclined to continue the contest.

He, however, withdrew his pretensions in favour of Mr. Charles Taylor, to whose merit he bore the most liberal testimony, in a speech delivered before the society on the 29th January, 1800.

Mr. Charles Taylor was elected secretary to the society, in which situation he remained until his death.

It is somewhat remarkable, that in the memorial from which some extracts have been given, Mr. Cartwright only slightly alludes to his improvements in the art of weaving; and in the enumeration of what he considered his most important inventions, that of weaving by machinery is altogether omitted, although it ultimately proved to be the only one that ever returned any portion of the expense incurred in bringing it to perfection. But it was unknown to him that the power-loom was gradually and secretly coming into use; and although he might not despair of its ultimate introduction, yet his patent-right being expired, all remuneration to himself for that invention seemed nearly hopeless.

The frequent invasions of his patent for combing wool, as well as the petitions that had been presented to parliament, as early as the year 1796, against the introduction of his machinery, might justly be considered as indications of its increasing importance, and rendered it, to all appearance, much more likely to prove advantageous than the weaving machine. But the difficulty of detection, as well as the expense of procuring redress, had paralyzed the efforts of his assignees, and had hitherto prevented them from pursuing inquiry in many cases in which they were morally convinced that great infringements on his patent-right were

practised. A most flagrant instance, however, having come to their knowledge, in
which the parties not only used machinery
on Mr. Cartwright's principles themselves,
but fabricated combing-machines for the use
of other manufacturers, an action was
brought, in the names of Major Cartwright
and his brother Charles, against the persons
thus offending.

In this cause, which came on to be tried
after Trinity term, 1799, the plaintiffs were
nonsuited; but this check, although an
addition to their expense and trouble, in no
way affected the principles on which they
sought redress. It appeared that when Mr.
Cartwright, in 1793, had assigned over his
patent-rights to his brothers, a suit was then
pending between him and another person
(on a question of invasion of patent-right),
and in the deed of assignment it was stipu-

lated that Mr. Cartwright should be held as legal owner of the patents, in trust for the assignees, until the suit in question should be legally determined. This suit had, in fact, terminated, not in a legal trial, but in one of those compromises to which the exigency of his affairs had but too frequently compelled Mr. Cartwright to agree; and his assignees, considering this compromise as having the same effect as if the matter had been determined by law, had consequently proceeded to act according to the different provisions of the assignment. The defendants, however, objected, that as no fresh assignment had taken place subsequent to the determination of the depending suit, the legal interest, not being vested in the plaintiffs, still remained in Edmund Cartwright, and therefore the defendants were entitled to recover. The learned judge (Rooke)

being of that opinion, directed a nonsuit.
But on the 18th November, of the same
year, Serjeant Runnington having moved to
set aside the nonsuit, the judge admitted,
that on a further consideration of the effect
of the deed than was given to it at Nisi
Prius, he was convinced "that the legal
interest vested in the plaintiffs immediately
on the determination of the suit that was
then depending at the time when the inden-
ture was executed." The rest of the court
having expressed an opinion to the same
effect, the nonsuit was set aside, and in the
following spring the cause was brought forward again, and tried before Lord Chief
Justice Eldon, in the Court of Common
Pleas.

The hardship of Mr. Cartwright's case,
so strongly appearing in the pains that had
been taken to evade his patents, and defeat

his efforts for protecting them, had awakened a general sympathy in his favour. The novelty and ingenuity of the machinery, of which he was clearly proved to be the inventor, with the great display of talent and knowledge on the part of those scientific persons who had been called upon as witnesses to distinguish between artful imitation and original invention, rendered this trial (John and Charles Cartwright *v.* Amatt and others) one of the most curious and interesting suits relative to the invasion of patent-right that had ever been brought forward in any court of justice. After a laborious investigation, which occupied the court two days, a verdict was given for the plaintiffs, with a thousand pounds damages.

The patient attention shewn by the Lord Chief Justice Eldon throughout the whole of this investigation, in which his lordship

I 3

took infinite pains to make himself master
of the mechanical part of the subject, was
always duly and gratefully acknowledged by
Major Cartwright and his brother.

So favourable an issue to this important
trial was naturally hailed by Mr. Cartwright
and his friends as the turning of the tide in
the state of his affairs.   It was discovered,
that in mills in several different parts of the
kingdom, his wool-combing machine had
been surreptitiously introduced and worked;
and now that he had legally substantiated
his claim to the invention, he might reasonably expect some pecuniary advantage from
its general adoption.   But, strange as it
may appear, no pecuniary benefit ever did
accrue to him connected with this invention,
either immediately, in consequence of this
trial, or subsequently, on obtaining an extension of his patent-right.   It cannot be

denied that Mr. Cartwright had, in the late trial, obtained the justice he was entitled to; but the expenses and difficulties attending it were such as to deter him from again seeking the same mode of redress. Major Cartwright, indeed, by his indefatigable perseverance, had succeeded in detecting fresh instances of piracy; but, in most instances, the assignees were induced to enter into compromise with their opponents, rather than incur the cost and vexation of another lawsuit; and in these compromises, it is hardly necessary to remark that Mr. Cartwright and his brothers were not likely to have the advantage. By this time, ten years of the patent-right (relative to wool-combing) were expired; and there seemed so little prospect of deriving a reasonable remuneration from it during the four remaining years, that Mr. Cartwright was advised to apply

to parliament for an extension of the term—
an indulgence, which, though rarely granted,
was not without example. He accordingly
presented a petition, to that effect, to the
House of Commons, on the 17th March,
1801, the substance of which is contained
in the following document, which, as it ex-
hibits in a succinct form, the causes of his
past and then existing difficulties, as well
as the grounds on which he sought parliamentary relief, is inserted nearly at full
length.

*" The Case of Edmund Cartwright, of Marylebone
Parish, Clerk, Master of Arts.*

" Mr. Cartwright, who now seeks the
protection of the legislature, is the author
of various mechanical inventions, of great
utility to the manufactures of his country;
but hitherto the labour of many anxious

years, fruitful in benefit to the public, hath brought him no other reward than barren reputation, accompanied by ruined fortunes, a situation bitterly aggravated by his having been obliged to behold many scandalous invasions of his property, without the means of resistance; and he might even have had torn from him the honour of having been the inventor of the art of combing long wool by machinery, had it not been for the assistance of friends, by whose means he was enabled to vindicate, in a court of law, the originality of that invention.

" Mr. Cartwright dates the origin of his misfortunes from the burning of a mill, which, in the year 1792, had been erected at Manchester, for the working of five hundred looms of his invention, which burning there was strong reason to believe had been the premeditated act of evil-minded persons.

Be this, however, as it may, it had the effect of deterring other manufacturers from attempting to adopt the use of the patent looms; notwithstanding the invention was such, that with the loom in question, one child of ten years old could execute as much as two experienced men, and in a style superior to any hand-weaving, which, at the best, is only an approximation towards correctness, whereas the patent loom gave the same number of threads to every yard of work, with mathematical accuracy.

" Notwithstanding, Mr. Cartwright, by the misfortune above mentioned, was totally defeated in his hope of advantage from an invention he was some years in bringing to perfection; yet the invention is still in possession of the public, and when the necessity of economy shall bring it into general use, the national profit, from its abridgment of labour, and superiority of work, cannot be less than *one million and a half sterling* per annum; especially as it will be the means, whenever universally adopted, of working up at home all that cotton twist and yarn, which now seeks a market in Saxony and other countries.

" But to come to the immediate subject of his present application to the legislature, Mr. Cartwright has to state, that although we derive from high antiquity the art of converting wool into jersey, by means of the ordinary comb, no one has recorded any improvement whatever, either upon the art or the implements, until they became the subject of his study and contemplation—a fact which affords no slight presumption of the inherent difficulty of the task.

" In the year 1790, Mr. Cartwright, however, after some abortive attempts, had the

happiness to strike out a practicable mode
of combing wool by machinery; and for the
combing machinery he then invented, together with other inventions, he obtained
his Majesty's patent for England, &c.
Pushing his experiments and discoveries,
he made successive improvements, taking
out a second patent in December of the
same year; and a third patent, for combing
machinery, and other inventions, in the
month of May, 1792, besides one in December, 1792, for Scotland.

" Fortunately for Mr. Cartwright, not
only the originality of his invention for
combing wool has been established upon a
rock, but its great national utility also has
been proved beyond contradiction, in the
course of the late laborious trial (which, for
two whole days, occupied the Court of Common Pleas), before the Right Honourable

Lord Chief Justice Eldon, and a special jury.

" As besides the presence of the Chief Justice, that trial was attended by a noble lord of the upper house, as a witness, and by an honourable member of the House of Commons, as a barrister; there are thus, in both houses of parliament, honourable and noble persons, to whom an appeal can be successfully made for the correctness of this statement. As the whole proceedings on that trial are very voluminous, Mr. Cartwright is printing, and means to publish, the summing up only, transcribed by Mr. Gurney, from his own short-hand notes, and the manuscript has been submitted to the Chief Justice for his correction. Therein will be seen the opinion Lord Eldon entertained, and frequently expressed, of the merit and utility of the invention. On the trial alluded to, it was proved, that by the use of each single set of Mr. Cartwright's patent combing machines, the saving in labour was more than one thousand one hundred pounds per annum; from which fact, combined with the estimate of the quantity of combing wool produced in England, it results that whenever the patent combing machine shall be universally adopted, the total saving to the nation cannot be so little as a million sterling a-year.

"Mr. Cartwright will not load his case with a detail of all those complicated causes which have hitherto prevented his deriving benefit from the invention in question; but leave them to the imagination of the reader, who will easily conceive the difficulty of stemming the tide of prejudice, rivalship, and injustice, by a man of ruined fortunes.

"Suffice it then to say, that after employing himself indefatigably for several years in his mechanical pursuits and discoveries, and failing to meet with that remuneration which could alone enable him to support the expense, he in the year 1793 sunk under a burthen too great for him to bear; surrendering for the benefit of his creditors, not only his whole estate, but assigning also all his patents themselves to trustees for the same purpose; and although the only rightful owner of the only valid patents for combing machines, he had the mortification to find himself, for seven years more, sinking deeper and deeper in debt, before even those patents could be put out of danger by the decision of a court of law.

" Why those patents, intrinsically of so much value as hath been stated, have not yet in any degree amended his pecuniary situation, is only to be accounted for from causes already touched upon, but the fact is certain, that the expense incurred in their preservation from that destruction of them that was attempted, has hitherto very far exceeded the profits they have brought in, so that by the necessary accumulation of a debt when there is not the means of keeping down the interest, the patentee is at this moment much deeper in debt than when he first surrendered his estates; whereas, had his patent combing machinery above mentioned, been adopted so early and so generally as he might reasonably have expected, he must long, ere now, have been in a state of affluence. The whole of his actual loss from prosecuting his mechanical inventions, when the debt thereby is taken into the account, much exceeds the sum of thirty thousand pounds. Seeing that the patents which included his wool-combing machinery are respectively drawing near to their expiration, while yet the degree in which the machines have been adopted is far too small to flatter the patentee with even a hope of paying the interest of his debt, unless the legislature shall generously take him under its protection; he has resolved to make the present application for an extension of the patent terms, so far as relates to the combing and preparing of wool. And he most humbly and earnestly hopes, that if his claims shall be found deserving, he shall receive from the individual and collective wisdom of parliament, that indulgence which other patentees, on similar applications, though not under circumstances of such peculiar hardship, have in many instances received from the legislature of their country."

The petition from Mr. Cartwright was favourably received by the House of Commons, and being referred to the consideration of a committee, different witnesses were examined, whose evidence went to prove not only the truth of all the allegations contained in the petition, but many additional circumstances calculated to strengthen the claims of the petitioner. It appeared by the evidence given on the occasion, by Major Cartwright, that by reason of the distressed state of the petitioner's affairs, he had not the means of appealing to the laws of his country for redress, but that he (the witness), as trustee for his brother's patent rights, had in the year 1799 commenced an action at law against certain invaders of those rights, which action was concluded in April, 1800, by a verdict in favour of the patentee.

Before it was convenient to him to advance
money in defence of the said patents, he
had found himself under the necessity, for
promoting the interests of the patentee and
his creditors, to make a compromise with
persons who had taken out two patents
for wool-combing machinery, although he
knew, and the parties themselves have
since acknowledged to him, that their
patents were for machinery that infringed
on the patents of the petitioner. It was
also stated by Major Cartwright, that his
brother had been compelled, by the exigency
of his affairs in 1793, to desist from a suit,
and enter into a compromise with another
person who had taken out a patent, which
the witness, having seen both the machinery
itself and a specification of it, was convinced
was not a valid patent, but an infringement of that of the petitioner. In conse-

quence of these forced compromises, and of
the inability, on the part of the inventor, to
vindicate in all cases of infringement the
originality of his invention, the public
remained in suspense as to what machine
for wool-combing might be legally and most
advantageously used; and this witness was
further of opinion, that unless the term of
the present patent-right should be reasonably prolonged, it would not be prudent for
the patentee, or his trustees, to enter into
any fresh lawsuit for the purpose of vindi-
cating his rights.

In addition to the above evidence, was
that of another witness, who had been employed for seven years in a mill, where six
sets of the combing machines were used;
and who estimated the profits arising
from each set at 1100*l.* per annum. This
witness mentioned also some other mills

where this machinery was employed, and was of opinion that, had it not been for the invasion of the patent, the original machine would have been in general use.

The report from the Committee, which was delivered the 13th April, by Mr. Spencer Stanhope, having proved satisfactory to the House, leave was given on the 8th May, to prepare and bring in a Bill, for the purpose of prolonging Mr. Cartwright's patent right, as far as regarded wool-combing, for the term of fourteen years. Whilst this Bill was in progress, several counter petitions were presented to the House from certain persons, who conceived that its operation would affect those agreements, or compromises, which Mr. Cartwright had been induced to enter into with them, as well as tend to check the ingenuity that

K

might be beneficially exercised in improving upon the invention in question.

These petitions being referred to the consideration of the Committee appointed to inquire into Mr. Cartwright's claims, and leave being given to the respective petitioners on both sides of the question to be heard by counsel, the matter was argued with all the acuteness that might be expected from some of the most eminent legal characters of the day. On this occasion, Mr. Cartwright conceiving himself personally aggrieved by the observations of one of the counsel for the opposing party, prepared a reply to these offensive observations, which, to judge from the sketch found amongst his papers, appears to have been drawn up with his usual perspicuity and clearness, though somewhat partaking of that indignant style, which, when roused by insult, it was well-known he could assume. The case of Mr. Watt, to whom an extension of patent right was granted in the fifteenth year of George III., having been alluded to, with an invidious comparison between his superior claims and those of Mr. Cartwright, the latter observed in reply, " It was admitted by the learned counsel of my opponent, that in extending the patent of Mr. Watt, Parliament was justified. Perhaps if the learned gentleman had known the whole of the two cases, he would not in the same breath have approved of the one extension, and condemned the other. The steam-engine is doubtless a machine of immense value, but Mr. Watt did not invent the steam-engine. That was a discovery of a former age. It had been known and used a great part of a century at the time when Mr. Watt first exercised his invention upon it, and his invention went no further than to an improvement. I do not mean to arrogate too much to myself, but I certainly have a right to say, that not only the first machines for combing wool were of my invention, but that I invented the very ART itself of combing by machinery, which till that time was utterly unknown, and in which I did not derive a single ray of light from any human ingenuity of a former date; and it will be kept in mind that the combing of wool is the very basis of the great supereminent manufacture of this country." On the 5th June, the Bill was read a third time, and passed the House of Commons. It received an amendment in the House of Lords, providing for the security of such persons as had previously entered into compromise with Mr. Cartwright, and on the 2nd July, the Bill received the Royal Assent.

This great object being attained, Mr. Cartwright, in having fourteen years of secured possession to look forward to, seemed placed in so advantageous a position, that it might reasonably be expected he should in future be able to treat with his opponents on more equitable terms, and compel those who employed his machinery to acknowledge a right thus sanctioned by an especial act of the Legislature. But the deficiency of pecuniary means to follow up the necessary inquiries, still continued; and in addition to this impediment, the activity of his mind became diverted towards a variety of other objects, from some of which he probably hoped to derive more immediate benefit. Whatever the causes of failure might be, it is certain that no advantage did accrue to him from the renewal of his patent right, nor indeed did he ever reap any pecuniary

gain from an invention of such acknowledged
ingenuity.*

* That the wool-combers had taken alarm at the
introduction of the machine in question, was evident
from the circumstance of there having been between
fifty and sixty petitions to Parliament against its
use as early as the year 1796.   The number of
wool-combers was estimated at fifty thousand.

CHAPTER VI.

In the interesting memoirs of Mr. Crabbe, the author, speaking of Dr. Cartwright, has, with great felicity of expression, noticed "the expanding versatility of his mind." This opinion was formed on the report of no common observer; and, indeed, the facility with which he could apply his mind to small, or rather familiar objects, was remarkable, and denoted its elasticity no less than its power. Frequent intercourse with men of ingenuity like himself, had led him into

a greater variety of speculations and experiments than it is necessary here to enumerate.
In the most common* arts of life, he could
seldom abstain from attempting some contrivance to reduce manual labour; at the
same time that he was far from being one of
those ingenious triflers who amuse themselves
in puerile contrivances, merely to exercise
their ingenuity without aiming at any useful
result. In agriculture, which had always
been one of his favourite pursuits, he was
continually devising some improvement, or
attempting some experiment. And that he

---

* In his own house bread was made by a machine,
and not many years since, an old friend of the family
going into a biscuit-maker's shop in Leeds, noticed
a machine that the man, who had been a navy biscuit-
maker, used for beating his dough. The man stated
that the machine was invented by a Mr. Cartwright,
of Doncaster, and that he should not know how to
get on with his business without it.

had at the same time an enlarged, and what
will probably be found to be, a just view of
the results of machinery, will appear from
the following extract from a letter addressed
to Sir John Sinclair, at that time President
of the Board of Agriculture, as early as the
year 1793, on the subject of a reaping-
machine which he was then engaged in constructing :—

"I am fully apprised that to many well-
intentioned men, looking only on the surface
of things, the invention I am preparing to
bring forward will appear as of an injurious tendency to the interests of the labouring poor. Were it possible to persuade
myself this would really be the case, it would
require no great stretch of benevolence to
suppress an invention of such pernicious
tendency; but unless the application of mechanism to the purposes of agriculture

should operate in a manner totally different from what it has uniformly done in manufactures, such apprehension must be groundless. It is a fact, indisputably ascertained by experience, that whatever facilitates labour multiplies the calls for it. Hence it is reasonable to conclude that reducing the expense, or giving expedition to the operations of industry, is eventually contributing to bring lands, hitherto uncultivated, into a state of cultivation, and occasioning those already in cultivation, to be cultivated more highly. Thus in agriculture, as in manufactures, it will be found that to enable one man, by the intervention of machinery, to do the work of ten, is not to throw nine men out of employment, as many would erroneously suppose, but on the contrary, it is to give one man ten pair of hands; and (which is of still greater consequence) with his powers of exertion, enlarging at the same time the field of his activity."

In June, 1801, he was adjudged a prize from the Board of Agriculture, for an Essay on Agriculture, composed with perspicuity and elegance; and which, though chiefly unfolding the general principles of the art, shews, at the same time, that the writer possessed an ample acquaintance with its detail.

About this period, a plan was in contemplation for establishing an experimental farm in the neighbourhood of London, under the direction of the Board of Agriculture, and Mr. Cartwright had been pointed out as a suitable person to superintend the management of it. Such an occupation would have been peculiarly agreeable to him, and his disappointment would have been great when the scheme was ultimately abandoned, had he not, shortly afterwards, received an offer from Francis, Duke of Bedford, to un-

dertake the direction of an experimental
farm that he was about to establish on his
own estate. His invention of the geometrical bricks had attracted the Duke's attention
as early as the year 1797, and the interest
he appeared to take in subjects connected
with agriculture, had still further recommended Mr. Cartwright to the notice of his
Grace, who was then distinguished ιs being
one of its most liberal patrons.

In the autumn of 1801, he entered on his
new engagement at Woburn; but in the
following spring, he had the misfortune of
losing his noble friend, whose untimely death,
not only cast a heavy gloom on Mr. Cartwright's own prospects, but contributed to
check that encouragement of agriculture, of
which his Grace had given so eminent an
example. The farming arrangements begun
by the late Duke at Woburn, were, however,
carried on by his successor, and Mr. Cart-

wright continued to reside there until the spring of 1807. During his residence in Bedfordshire, his time and attention were chiefly applied to subjects connected with agriculture; but that pursuit, when conducted on a liberal scale, leads to a variety of other objects which naturally bring inquiring minds into contact with each other. The short period of peace which Europe at that time enjoyed, facilitated the communication amongst each other of men of science in different countries, and Mr. Cartwright had the gratification of finding that his name was not unknown to persons of that description on the continent, several of whom sought his acquaintance, on taking advantage of the peace to visit England.

In 1803 he was adjudged the silver medal from the Society of Arts, for the invention of a three-furrow plough. In 1804 he was chosen an honorary member of the Board of Agriculture, and in 1805 received the gold medal from the same society.

The essay for which the Board of Agriculture had awarded him the medal, contains a minute detail of some curious experiments on the application and fertilizing effects of different substances used as manure; and as the experiments were conducted with great exactitude, the author seems fully justified in the inferences he derives from them. But feeling some degree of diffidence as to the correctness of his own conclusions, he appears, from the following letters, to have submitted his manuscript to the revision of that eminent philosopher, Sir Humphry Davy:—

MR. CARTWRIGHT TO SIR HUMPHRY DAVY.

" MY DEAR SIR,—I herewith send you a detail of the experiments I have been trying on manures. I fear you will find it very imperfect. Business, which was not to be dispensed with, and ill health, which, in the course of last summer, blotted out nearly three months of my existence, have compelled me to compress what I have written into a very small compass. I say not this, however, as an apology to you, to whom a word will sufficiently explain my meaning, but many words are required to make even the clearest ideas intelligible to common apprehensions. " *Verbum sapienti, insipienti volumen.*" As I mean this paper, in some shape or other, and at no very distant period, to meet the public eye, you will have the goodness to look it over for the rectifying any error, whether chemical or not, which you may perceive in it. I will thank you also for any observations which the perusal of it may suggest to you.

" You will observe I have not mentioned to whom I have been indebted for the analyzing the earth, as I do not think it justifiable to

speak of private communications without
permission.   I hope, however, that I shall
have your permission, not only to mention
this, but many other valuable communications I shall receive from you.   As soon as
you have had time to look over the MS.
and to note down your remarks on the blank
pages, I will thank you to return it, &c.

"EDMUND CARTWRIGHT."

SIR HUMPHRY DAVY TO MR. CARTWRIGHT.

"DEAR SIR,—I have perused your treatise twice with very great pleasure, and I
hope you will soon make it public.

"The only point of theory in which I differ
from you, is where you attribute the effect
of salt to its power of attracting moisture
from the air.   This agency must be very
slight, and I should rather conceive that
the benefit derived, must depend upon the
saline matter being taken into the organs

of the plants. Muriate of soda is found in a great number of plants, and it may be one of the substances contributing to their healthy organization.

" I have not the slightest objection to your bringing forward the analysis on my authority. And I feel proud in having been able, even in so slight a degree, to assist your very important researches.

" I am, dear Sir, &c.,

" H. DAVY.

" London, Feb. 21, 1805."

That portion of the experiments above referred to, which relate to the efficacy of salt as a manure, are described in a paper ublished in the " Philosophical Magazine,' vol. xxiii. p. 16. But as the application of chemistry to agriculture is a subject which attracts much attention at the present day, it has been thought advisable to print the entire essay. [See Appendix (F).] Independently of the great care with which these experiments appear to have been conducted, the treatise derives a further value, from the notes appended to the original MS. by Sir Humphry Davy, and now first published.

In 1806, he also received from the Board a silver medal for an essay on the culture of potatoes. In the same year he took the degree of Dr. in Divinity, and officiated as domestic chaplain to the Duke of Bedford. In 1807 he published a small volume of letters and sonnets addressed to Lord John Russel, whose character and talents even at an early age, had engaged Dr. Cartwright's sincere admiration and esteem. The sonnet seemed always to have been a favourite form of composition with him, and he gives in the introductory letter this humorous and characteristic reason for his preference, that it is " a species of composition admirably suited to the resources of a super-

annuated poet, whose brains will not bear
more than fourteen strokes of the poetical
pump, before the reservoir is exhausted."
With greater justice than he measures to
himself, it may be allowed that the sonnet
entitled Sympathy, indicates no exhaustion
of feeling, any more than the Climacteric
Thoughts do, the approach of superan-
nuation.

SYMPATHY.

That law of nature well may we admire,
  Which gives to matter sympathies profound:
  Touch but the simple string when duly wound,
An echo answers from its kindred wire.
But greater reverence must that law inspire,
  Which mind obeys, when rightly tuned and sound,
  Each selfish tone in SYMPATHY is drown'd,
That makes the heart her animated lyre.
  If sympathy, her kindred touch impart,
  What chords of passion vibrate through the heart!
What notes within her diapason lie!
No strain of woe too deep, of joy too high!
She tunes in unison each mental strife,
And hence the moral harmony of life.

CLIMACTERIC THOUGHTS.

Now threescore years and three have pass'd away,
And time and care have turn'd these locks to grey;
Old age, and death, with slow, yet certain pace,
Creep on to terminate my mortal race;
And lo! to make their visit more severe,
What horrid phantoms in their train appear!
What dire diseases press upon my view,
Of every shapeless form and squalid hue!
See Fever, gasping with volcanic breath,
And Ague, colder than the hand of death!
Eroding Cancer, that evades the light,
And Dotage, drivelling on in mental night!
With agonizing throes, see Phrenzy rave,
And Dropsy struggling in a watery grave!
Her helpless victim stretch'd upon the rack,
With ruthless blade, see Gout prepares the attack!
To every vital part she turns the point,
And drives a fiery wedge thro' every joint.
Last in the gloomy rear see Palsy stand,
With trembling grasp to shake life's lingering sand!
All these, and more, alas! too well I see
On human life attend by Heaven's decree.
May then, that Heaven to whose decree I kneel,
Teach me to bear what all are born to feel;
Give me, as hitherto, thro' trials past,
A patient mind, unshaken to the last!

CHAPTER VII.

It has been already stated, that Dr. Cartwright, even during the existence of his patent right, had retained but little expectation of deriving any pecuniary advantage from his invention of weaving; and when his latest patent had been several years expired, the prospect of remuneration appeared entirely hopeless. He might be aware that his loom was coming into use, but he had now so little communication with the manufacturing districts, that he could form no idea of the extent to which it was adopted. Weaving by machinery was, however, beginning to make considerable progress, and was even then preparing for him the only compensation that he ever received for years of anxiety, and great pecuniary loss. This progress was connected with the circumstances of the times, by which an extraordinary impulse had been given to the British manufactures in general, and which rendered the beginning of the present century a far more favourable period for the introduction of machine weaving than that in which Dr. Cartwright had first attempted it. The great improvements that had been effected in the art of spinning, had, with other causes, occasioned a vast accumulation of cotton yarn, which on account of the disturbed state of the Continent, could no longer be disposed of in the foreign market, neither could hands (which, in consequence of a long protracted war, were become less numerous than they had been) be found sufficient to work it up at home. At the same time, the demand for English cotton piece goods was greatly increasing, and the manufacturers found themselves called upon to devise some means of answering a demand which want of hands and want of looms prevented their being able to supply.* The only expedient that seemed to present itself, was the adoption of the hitherto rejected powerloom: thus literally justifying the hypothetical suggestion of its author, in that remarkable conversation which had first turned his attention to the subject of mechanics.† From the year 1792, when Messrs. Grimshaw's mill had been destroyed,

* See Radcliffe on Cotton Spinning, p. 12.
† See p. 56, *supra*.

and Mr. Cartwright's establishment, at
Doncaster, as well as some others connected
with it, was abandoned, it does not appear
that any manufacturer had ventured openly
to employ his loom, liable as he would in
that case have been to a payment for its
use during the existence of the patent right.
The machine, however, had not been lost
sight of, and on its becoming open to the
public by the expiration of the patent;
several manufacturers sought to adapt it to
their own purposes. Great improvements
it doubtless did receive from that ingenuity
and spirit of enterprise, which were called
into action by the circumstances of the
times, but rather unfairly towards Dr.
Cartwright,* some of these improvers as-

---

* Mr. Peter Marsland was a most honourable
exception to this remark; though he had been himself a great improver of the power-loom, yet he was

sumed to themselves the whole merit of the invention, and though his machine formed the basis, as it still does, of all the power-looms that have hitherto been found effective, his claim to the original invention was far from being generally recognised. In some instances the invention had been ascribed to persons who had formerly worked looms under a licence from Dr. Cartwright, but who, either from want of capital, or the then unfavourable state of the trade, had not succeeded in their undertakings, and yet had retained so decided a conviction of the value of the machine as to be induced to revive it under more encouraging auspices.

The improved quality of the yarn had also contributed to render machine weaving

so fully satisfied of the justice of Mr. Cartwright's claim, that his name stands first in the memorial presented to Government in his favour.

L

less difficult, as well as the fabric produced by it, of a more perfect quality than when Dr. Cartwright first undertook it. The extraordinary advances that had been made in the application of mechanical power, by improvements in the steam-engine &c., doubtless facilitated the extension of the power-loom; but in justice to a most ingenious man, it must be acknowledged that Mr. Radcliffe's admirable contrivance for dressing the warp* *before* it is put into the loom, by which means time and attendance are saved, contributed probably beyond any other improvement to render it completely available.† About the year 1806, Dr.

---

* That is, applying paste to render the threads smooth.

† " The great obstacle to the success of the power-loom was, that it was necessary to stop the machine frequently in order to dress the warp as it unrolled from the beam, which operation required a man to

Cartwright was induced to make some inquiries respecting the state of the cotton manufacture in general, but more especially in the neighbourhood and town of Man-

be employed for each loom, so that there was no saving of expense. This difficulty was happily removed by the invention of an extremely ingenious and effectual mode of dressing the warp before it was placed in the loom."—*Baines' History of the Cotton Manufacture*, p. 231.

It should appear, however, that Mr. Radcliffe's mode of dressing the warp is equally applicable to the hand-loom. In his "Origin of Power-loom Weaving," p. 30, he says, "Though at that time I was obliged to bring such a number of boys and girls into the factory to work the looms, yet when the hands had been taught to work them, it was my intention to disperse all these looms into the cottages of the weavers throughout the country, in lots proportioned to the number of children in the families, delivering them the warps ready dressed, and prepared ready for weaving off the beam, and their weft in cops ready for the shuttle, without previous winding."

L 2

chester, and found that machine-weaving
was already practised to a much greater
extent than he had anticipated, and that
considerable profit was accruing, not only
to individuals, but to the country at large;
from discoveries which to him had been
productive of nothing but loss and disappointment.   In a letter to his friend Dr.
Bardsley, senior, an eminent physician in
Manchester, he could not refrain from expressing the bitterness of his feelings on the
subject, and this letter being communicated
to some highly respectable and influential
gentlemen of that place, they were so much
struck by the hardship of Dr. Cartwright's
case, as to express their willingness to con-
cur in any application to Parliament that
he or his friends should think proper to
make, for the purpose of obtaining some
remuneration from the public.   In conse-

quence of the encouragement given by these gentlemen, Dr. Bardsley, with a warmth of friendship most truly appreciated by him in whose favour it was exerted, applied himself to obtain the information that was required, in order to shew the grounds on which Dr. Cartwright might have a claim to public gratitude, and also what was no less material, to satisfy the minds of the manufacturers that he really was the original inventor of the machine in question, which so many of them were in the habit of using.

The result of these inquiries tended to shew, that the power loom was already employed to a considerable extent, and that its use was rapidly increasing; but no stronger proof could be required of the importance that was attached to its progress by those best acquainted with, and most deeply concerned in the trade, than the fact, that a

memorial, in Dr. Cartwright's favour, was
signed by fifty of the most respectable and
influential gentlemen of the town and neighbourhood of Manchester, and presented to
Government in August, 1807.* This memorial was followed, in the spring of 1808, by a
petition from Dr. Cartwright, to the House
of Commons; and the house having agreed to
take his claims into consideration, a committee was appointed to that effect; and on
the 4th and 7th March, and on the 12th
April, evidence was examined in support
of his allegations. He was fortunately
enabled to bring forward a very material witness in Mr. Joseph Taylor, who
had not only been his own engineer at the
outset of his mechanical career, but had also
been the superintendant at Messrs. Grimshaw's factory, at Knott Mill, at the time

* See Appendix G.

when its destruction by fire had given so
severe a check to the introduction of the
power-loom. In Mr. Baines's interesting History of the Cotton Manufacture, is a passage
relative to Messrs. Grimshaw's connection
with Dr. Cartwright, which might lead to
a very different inference from what really
was the fact, and which can only have found
a place in a work of so much candour and
liberality, in consequence of some defective
information. It is here stated, that "about
1790, Messrs. Grimshaw, of Gorton, under
a licence from Dr. Cartwright, erected a
weaving factory at Knott Mills, Manchester,
and *attempted to improve the power-loom*,
at great cost to themselves. *They did not
succeed*, and the factory being burnt down,
they abandoned the undertaking."—p. 231.
Now, Messrs. Grimshaw had certainly been
at a great expense, but that was incurred in

erecting a factory, which was to contain
500 of Dr. Cartwright's looms; and as only
about four-and-twenty of the looms were
actually set to work, before the mill was
destroyed, no just estimate could be formed
of the probable success of the undertaking, although it appears from Taylor's
evidence, that the looms (which there is
no ground whatever for supposing Messrs.
Grimshaw had been at any cost to improve,)
were found to do their work remarkably
well.

The substance of Mr. Taylor's evidence
was to this effect. He stated, that he was
acquainted with Dr. Cartwright's invention,
in 1784, even before the first patent was
taken out; that he had then seen a trial of
it, and, in his judgment, it was calculated
to answer the purpose of weaving. In 1791,
he had accompanied Mr. Grimshaw, who

was a master check-manufacturer, in great business, to Doncaster, where he then witnessed the improvements Mr. Cartwright had effected since the taking out of his first patent. Mr. Grimshaw having entered into an agreement to employ a certain number of Mr. Cartwright's looms, proceeded to build a large mill for that purpose; the expense of which, independently of the steam-engine and machinery, which would be nearly 3000*l*. additional, was estimated at 5700*l*. Of the four-and-twenty looms that were completed, twelve were set to work, at weaving check, which had been Mr. Grimshaw's peculiar line of business. These looms worked exceedingly well; they wrought the work for half the amount of wages which they were then paying to hand weavers; the weavers, in consequence, threatened to destroy the mill, and the owners received anonymous* letters to that effect. On receiving these letters, a considerable part of the property, especially the yarn, was removed out of the mill; and in about a month afterwards, in March, 1792, it was burnt down. From the rapidity with which the building was consumed, it probably was fired in different places, and Mr. Taylor was confirmed, in his conviction, of its being by design, from the circumstance of there not having been, to his personal knowledge as manager, any fire employed within the mill during three preceding days.

* One of these letters (copied from the advertisement issued under the signature of the Right Honourable Henry Dundas, then one of his Majesty's principal Secretaries of State, dated Whitehall, March 22nd, 1792, offering a reward to discover the offender), was in the following terms :—

"SIRS—We have sworn together to destroy your factory, if we die for it, and to have your life for ruining our trade ; and if you go on, you know the certainty, which comes unknown to my companions."

Messrs. Grimshaw, who had ensured their property to the amount of 12,000*l.*, did not venture to re-build their mill at Manchester, and had tried in vain in other places. It also appeared in evidence, that the alarm, in consequence of this untoward event, and continued threats on the part of the hand-weavers, had become so general, that no one ventured openly to use the loom within the period of Dr. Cartwright's patent right. One passage in Mr. Taylor's evidence seems particularly deserving of notice, as it shews, if his opinion be correct, *that this machine is not necessarily chargeable with all the evils that have fallen on the hand-loom weavers, and that if they had availed themselves of its advantages, instead of obstinately setting themselves against it, the great manufacturers might not have been driven to adopt the mill system to the* *extent they have done: and that the hand-weavers might still have retained such a portion of business in their own hands as would have enabled them better to meet those fluctuations which every description of trade and manufactures is liable to, and which legislative interference cannot prevent, and only very imperfectly remedy.* On being desired to state to the committee whether the unavoidable effect of this invention is to crowd the persons together who are employed in it, Mr. Taylor replied, that " the machinery may be worked with equal advantage without crowding people together, by the weaver having looms in his own family and turning them by hand; six looms may be turned by one man, by which means he may employ little children, and superintend them himself, and will have six looms at once, instead of one, and every loom would do as much work as one weaver would do at a common loom."

It was also stated by Mr. Taylor, that cloth, woven by machinery, was of a better quality and bore a higher price than that woven by hand; a statement fully confirmed by the fact, that cloth woven by hand is frequently stamped as power-loom cloth, and sold as such to all parts of the world.*

* See Radcliffe, Origin of Power Loom Weaving. "The superiority of machine cloth may easily be accounted for. The best hand-weavers seldom produce a piece of uniform evenness; indeed, it is next to impossible for them to do so, because a weaker or stronger blow with the lathe immediately alters the thickness of the cloth; and after an interruption of some hours, the most experienced weaver finds it difficult to re-commence with a blow of precisely the same force as the one with which he left off. In steam looms the lathe gives a certain steady blow, and when once regulated by the engine, moves with the greatest precision from the beginning to the end

The next evidence was that of Mr.
William Radcliffe, of Stockport, a gentleman of great practical experience and knowledge in every branch of the cotton trade,
and whose opinion as to the probable increase of the use of the power-loom, has been
completely justified by the event. Until
applied to by Dr. Cartwright's solicitors, it
does not appear that Mr. Radcliffe knew
who was the inventor of the power-looms,
though he had himself employed them; but
the circumstance of these looms being known
by the name of the *Doncaster loom*, sufficiently identified the inventor, and Mr.
Radcliffe came forward, with the utmost

of the piece. Cloth made by these looms, when
seen by those manufactures who employ hand-
weavers, at once excites admiration and a conscious-
ness that their own work cannot exceed it."—*Guest's
Hist. Cotton Manufacture*, p. 46.

liberality and candour, to do justice to their merit. His evidence, in the first place, went to shew that the inveterate opposition of the hand-weavers had been the means of deterring the manufacturers from adopting the use of machinery, until the trade had now become such that the hand-weavers themselves were interested in producing a sufficient supply of cotton goods at home to answer the increasing demand for them, as well as to work up the surplus quantity of yarn. "During a period of about nine years," Mr. Radcliffe said, "from 1793 to 1802, the machinery for spinning cotton yarn, with the ingenuity, practical knowledge, and persevering industry of the persons concerned in this branch, became so perfect as to enable the spinners to produce more yarn than could possibly be made into cloth by all the weavers Great Britain could collect for the purpose. The demand for cotton cloth was equal, during this period, to take off the whole produce of the spindle, if weavers could have been found to have made it into cloth; but this being impossible, the spinners began to export the surplus to the manufacturers abroad—into France, Germany, Russia, Switzerland, Holland, Spain, Portugal, Denmark, Sweden, &c., countries possessing a multitude of weavers formerly employed in weaving linen, silk, stuffs, &c. &c., whose labour was to be had at half the price which was paid for such labour in this country. The consequence of which has been, that these foreign manufacturers began to furnish their neighbours with such cotton cloths as heretofore they could only obtain from this country: hence, by degrees, the British manufacturers and the East India Company lost nearly all their trade for piece goods to those countries before mentioned, which is the sole cause of all the distress which is now heard of in the cotton trade." Mr. Radcliffe proceeded to state, that "this invention of Dr. Cartwright's, coupled with some other improvements that have been lately discovered for preparing and dressing the cotton twist ready for the loom, is particularly calculated to remedy this evil speedily, by working up a great part of their surplus yarn, and that not into fabrics that will interfere with the cotton goods heretofore made by our weavers, but into vast quantities of strong stout cotton goods for shirting, sheeting, &c." He also stated, that he knew many spinners who were ready to appropriate part of their mills to weaving by machinery, on Dr. Cartwright's principles, when any demand for piece goods should spring up; and that if it should be generally adopted, the trade for piece goods would immediately revive, and by degrees the markets would not only open again for cotton goods manufactured in Great Britain, but also for those imported by the East India Company, who had suffered very greatly by the foreigners making from our twist, goods similar to what they used to purchase at the Company's sales, which had answered their purpose abroad as a substitute for India cloth." Mr. Radcliffe added, " that he considered the invention of Dr. Cartwright as so important to the prosperity of the Manchester trade, that were it suppressed, or its application no further extended, the cotton trade would be chiefly confined to spinning, and the weavers on the continent, in the end, become the sole manufacturers." On being asked what were the number of mills in which these looms were set up, he replied that he knew of twenty-eight, or thirty, and there might be more of which he did not know; and also gave it as his opinion, that it had been necessary for Dr. Cartwright to establish a manufactory, and to have a number of looms actually at work, in order to shew their operation, and to try different experiments for the purpose of bringing them to perfection.

We cannot close this portion of our subject without some expression of sympathy for the hard lot of the unfortunate Mr. Radcliffe. His great ingenuity and services to the country deserved a better return than the neglect and discouragement he experienced; and he, alas! was one of those instances of unrewarded talents that have solely contributed to the aggrandizement of others. The author was in correspondence, some years since, with Mr. Radcliffe, on the

subject of this memoir, and was much gratified by the candour and liberality with
which he did ample justice to the value of
Dr. Cartwright's invention. It was painful
to learn that he had himself reaped so little
advantage from improvements that had
greatly facilitated the use of the power-
loom; and it was no less painful to feel conscious of the utter inability to forward and
assist his claims to national remuneration.

From other evidence brought forward, it
appeared that Dr. Cartwright had expended
between thirty and forty thousand pounds
in prosecuting and bringing his mechanical
inventions to perfection.

In the following year, a grant of ten
thousand pounds was made, on the part of
His Majesty's government, to Dr. Cartwright,
"for the good service he had rendered the
public by his invention of weaving."

It cannot be inconsistent with a liberal economy for a government to encourage ingenuity, which for want of support might be lost to the public; at the same time a government ought not to be called upon to indemnify individuals for losses and expenditure incurred in speculations, which (though eventually advantageous to the public) had been undertaken solely with a view of profit to themselves. But in the instance of Dr. Cartwright, *compensation*, rather than *remuneration*, was the principle on which he sought the attention of the legislature. A system of intimidation, against which the laws of his country had failed to protect him, had, for a series of years, prevented a fair trial being made of his machinery for weaving; and, in addition to the disappointment of his reasonable expectations of gain, a prejudice had also been created against the invention itself, which

nothing but an extraordinary combination
of circumstances could finally have overcome. This prejudice had a tendency to
deprive him of the credit of the invention.
It had been hastily concluded that the
machine was inefficient, because it had not
been adopted; and when, on being tried, it
was found to succeed, its success was attributed wholly to the alterations engrafted
upon it. Indeed, there is great reason to
believe, that but for this public recognition
from the legislature, Dr. Cartwright's claim,
even to the invention of the power-loom,
would not have been generally admitted,
although at the time of his application to
parliament there does not appear to have
been the slightest attempt made to invali-
date his claim to originality on the part of
those to whom the chief merit of the invention has subsequently been ascribed.

Admitting, however, that the grant to Dr. Cartwright was conferred as a reward to ingenuity, it ought, in justice to those members of His Majesty's Government who proposed it, to be observed, that it was not incautiously or lightly made. It was not until two years after the presentation to the first lord of the Treasury, of the memorial from Manchester, that Mr. Perceval proposed in the House of Commons any remuneration to Dr. Cartwright; and he, in the meantime, had been required to produce satisfactory evidence in support of his allegations, whilst to his rivals, or opponents, ample opportunity had been given to rebut them.

The gratitude with which Dr. Cartwright received this act of justice, was heightened by the reflection that he owed it to the liberal feelings of a ministry, to whose leading members he was personally unknown, but to whom it was not unknown that his principal associates and connexions were chiefly amongst their political opponents.

The event has more than justified the view which the legislature of 1809 was led to form of the importance of the invention of the power-loom. The warmest advocate for mechanical enterprise, the most sanguine believer in its success, could hardly have anticipated that more than one hundred thousand power-looms should be employed in the island of Great Britain alone. Yet such, at the present time, is the astonishing fact; and these looms, now brought, by the incessant application of ingenuity, to an extreme degree of perfection, are producing yearly millions of pieces of almost every variety of fabric that can be applied to the useful or ornamental clothing of mankind.

CHAPTER VIII.

HAVING received the sum awarded by parliament, and being now sixty-six years of age, Dr. Cartwright was anxious to pass the remainder of his life in retirement and tranquillity; and having decided on settling in Kent, he purchased a small farm at Hollanden, situated between Sevenoaks and Tunbridge. At this place he spent the last years of his existence, amusing himself with various experiments in agriculture, chemistry, and mechanics, and occupied, to the

M

utmost of his ability, in promoting the welfare of his fellow-creatures.

To the poor he was always a kind and judicious adviser, and as a magistrate, able and enlightened. His friendly assistance in the church was always at the service of the neighbouring clergy; and we may be allowed in this place to remark, that his manner of performing his clerical duties was truly solemn and impressive.

In society no man was ever more popular; his conversation, full of information, conveyed in a lively and pleasing manner, was entirely free from assumption or dogmatism; and the kindness and simplicity of his deportment made his company agreeable to all, especially to the young, for whom, in common with many other men of superior genius and attainments, he had a particular predilection. In the " Life of Crabbe," (vol. i.

pp. 135, 136,) there is a very appropriate description of Dr. Cartwright, which is the more remarkable, as it shews the impression he made on the writer, then a child of six or seven years old:—" During my father's residence at Stratherne," says the Rev. George Crabbe, " and also at his other country places, he very rarely paid or received visits except in his clerical capacity; but there was one friend, whose expanding versatility of mind and rare colloquial talents made him a most welcome visitor, and he was a frequent one. I allude to Dr. Edmund Cartwright, a poet and mechanist of no small eminence, who at this period was the incumbent of Goadby, and occasionally lived there, though his principal residence was at Doncaster, where vast machines were worked under his direction. Few persons could tell a good story so well—no man could

make more of a trite one. I can just remember him; the portly, dignified old
gentleman of the last generation—grave
and polite, but full of humour and spirit."

About 1809, Dr. Cartwright communicated to the Board of Agriculture an account
of some experiments on the effects of sugar
in fattening sheep. He gave to fifteen
sheep four ounces of sugar each per diem,
mixed with other food, and in the short
space of twenty-eight days found that, on
the average, they had increased one-fifth in
weight, and that two of them had gained
upwards of one-fourth. He suggested that
the duty might be deducted on sugar thus
applied, and that to protect the revenue,
the sugar might be rendered useless for other
purposes by mixing it with linseed, palm, or
train oils, assafœtida, charcoal, or other substances, which, though nauseous to the

human palate, were found not to diminish the zest with which the sheep devoured the sugar.   He thus sums up his conclusions :—

" 1. That sugar may be given with great advantage to sheep, if not confined, especially if they have access to green food, however small in quantity.

" 2. That sugar may be given to them, with every prospect of a beneficial effect, in the quantity of four ounces per day to each sheep.

" 3. That sugar, supposing it to be purchased at 4d. per lb. (which it might be, if duty free), would, at the rate of four ounces per day, be paid for in a return of flesh, exclusive of the advantage of expeditious feeding, and the benefit to be derived from the manure.

" 4. That six ounces per day to each sheep exceeds the maximum that can be given with the best advantage.

" 5. That the advantage of stall-feeding sheep altogether upon sugar and dry food, of whatever nature that food may be, is extremely problematical."

From this period of Dr. Cartwright's residence at Hollanden, his mechanical pursuits were chiefly speculative, and his habits those of a retired rather than a practical philosopher; yet there is abundant proof that the rust of old age never settled on his brilliant faculties, and a few extracts from his letters will shew the constant vigour and activity, as well as that singular elasticity and cheerfulness of spirit, which years of disappointment and anxiety had failed to extinguish or repress.

Among his chief correspondents was his old friend, Dr. Pearson, an eminent physician, particularly distinguished for his knowledge of chemistry, to whom he addressed the following playful invitation, which, like all his poetical effusions, was composed with a readiness and facility almost entitling them to be considered as extemporaneous :—

"4th June, 1812.

"For one short day the world forego,
  Its noise and cares and follies flee—
That short unclouded day bestow
  On friendship, solitude, and me.

"For you my Susan shall provide
  A barn-door fowl, a brace of fish,
And, what was once old England's fare,
  Roast beef on a galvanic dish.

"Though with no costly viands graced,
  Disdain not then my board to share;
Wine, suited to your classic taste,
  Shall compensate for homely fare.

"The Teian grapes' nectarious juice
  That once Anacreon quaffed, is mine:
Were mine the power, I would produce
  Anacreon's wit as well as wine.

"And yet, who knows what wine may do?
　　Wine might Anacreon's wit supply;
　Tipsy, he might have rivall'd you—
　　When sober, been as dull as I."

" TO DR. PEARSON.

" 1st Jan. 1814.

" As you tell me you set a value on what
I send you, here then, *nostrorum candide
judex*, follows—

"A BIRTHDAY SOLILOQUY AT SEVENTY.

" To fame and to fortune adieu!
　　The toils of ambition are o'er;
　Let folly these phantoms pursue,
　　I now will be cheated no more.

"Resignation be mine, and repose,
　　So shall life be unclouded at last;
　And while I prepare for its close
　　I will think, with a smile, on the past.

" Yet, as to this world must be given
　　Some part of life's limited span,
　The thoughts that ascend not to Heaven
　　I'll give to the service of man."

" TO THE REV. GEORGE CRABBE.

" 30th Aug. 1817.

" MY DEAR SIR,—In rummaging over an old magazine, I learned that your son, and, I presume, my godson, was married to one of the belles of Trowbridge. I need not say, that both he and you, and the lady of his choice, have all of you my best wishes and congratulations. I had lately a letter from my old friend and neighbour, Thomas Shaw, of Waltham, who tells me his family consists of seven children, all doing and likely to do well, and that they have presented him with as many grandchildren. I have at present ten, and expect an increase every day. You will be reckoning your treasures of this sort soon; as such riches increase, we may be permitted to set our affections upon them. I saw, by the papers, that you were one of the officiating priests of Apollo

at the apotheosis of Kemble; the ode which
was recited, and which contained a few brilliant stanzas, was attributed to Campbell.
I have seen two or three short extracts from
Lalla Rookh, which were exquisite; the
whole poem, I shall probably not see; two
guinea volumes are above my purchase, and
I live so retired and unconnected with literary society, that I see no books but what
I buy. Have you published anything lately?
If you have, let me know it. I have made
great additions to my prophetic epistle; but
before I have an opportunity of publishing
it, the events it foretels will become matter
of history."

" TO SIR STAMFORD RAFFLES.

"Feb. 2, 1819.

" Availing myself of the permission you
gave me, in the letter I had the honour of

receiving from you on your departure from Portsmouth for Sumatra, I again address you, on the subject of transporting into your own country the seeds of such plants as there is a probability of being naturalized here, and as are likely to be useful in the garden, especially the cottager's garden, or in agriculture. And here I must observe, that the seeds of plants already known and cultivated will be acceptable, as they may be the means of introducing new and improved varieties, even though they be the seeds of plants originally transported from Europe. Vegetables, like animals, after a very few years of naturalization, will acquire from their new situation new habits and propensities, which, as it may happen, will be more or less valuable than the parent stock that they were derived from. This I know from experience. Four or five years

ago I was indebted to the kindness of Lord
Charles Somerset for some garden seeds
from the Cape, almost all of which were
evidently of European extraction, and yet
the greater part of them differed, and most
of them for the better, from those of the
same family here. Early ripening, in articles of field culture, is a great desideratum
in this climate, in which the hopes of the
agriculturist are frequently disappointed by
a late and protracted harvest. Precocity,
I have observed, is one of the properties
which plants generally acquire by having
had a removal into a warmer climate than
that of which they are natives, and which
they retain after they are brought back.
Again, even those plants which are common
to every country, and partake of the same
nature, will arrive at maturity at an earlier
or later period, accordingly as they are cul-

tivated in a climate and soil more or less genial; and this disposition they will retain, for a few years at least, under very unfavourable circumstances. These considerations make me wish for specimens of wheat, peas, beans, vetches, &c., if such are to be met with; as also seeds of such grasses as appear to be hardy and productive, and thrive in cool situations. You will now perceive, sir, what my ideas and wishes are relative to the matters I have stated. You will confer a lasting obligation upon me, and eventually, I trust, on the public, in whose service I am labouring, by furnishing me with a very small packet of seeds (a pint of each, more or less, would be sufficient) of such plants as you think may be beneficially introduced into the British Isles.

" I am well aware that by most men in your situation, a request like the present would be deemed both obtrusive and impertinent; but I am under no such apprehensions from you, and if I rightly understand your character, it will be some satisfaction to you to contribute to the innocent gratification of an individual, even though a stranger to you. Wishing, however, to be in some degree known to you, not personally—my advanced age precluding that expectation—yet by something, at least, that I have done, I have some pleasure in acquainting you, that in the course of my agricultural experiments last summer, I had the singular good fortune to discover an absolute remedy for the mildew in wheat—cheap, and of easy application. I need not point out to you the incalculable benefit this discovery must be of, both to the growers of wheat and to every individual consumer of that indispensable article of human food; our defective crops being more frequently occasioned by mildew than by all other causes combined.

" The intelligence of your spirited remonstrances and protest against the aggressions of the Dutch reached England a few posts ago, and were yesterday the subject of discussion in the House of Lords. That your conduct, on this occasion, has added to the great estimation in which your name is already held, you will learn from higher authority than mine. From the loose manner in which our diplomatists have drawn up the treaty between this country and the Netherlands, there is reason to fear that the native princes of Java will not be suffered to realize the prospects of happiness and independence which your humane and enlightened policy had taught them to look forward to.

" I am, Sir, &c. &c.,

" EDMUND CARTWRIGHT.

" P.S.—Since you left England, the forgery of bank-notes has increased to an alarming degree, in consequence of which, during the last session of parliament, a committee was appointed to inquire into the best means of preventing it. I, amongst others, suggested an idea to them, which I thought might answer the purpose. My suggestion was, for the Bank to send a confidential paper-maker of their own into the East Indies, who, combining his own knowledge and secrets of the art with the practice of the East, operating upon materials unknown in Europe, might produce a paper most difficult of imitation, and which would differ so much from paper manufactured here, as to be distinguishable from it at first sight."

" TO MAJOR CARTWRIGHT.

"24th April, 1819.

" MY DEAR BROTHER,—In a letter which
I received some time ago, from a friend in
London, I was told that he had lately seen
you, and that he thought you did not look
so well as usual; but as I have received two
or three letters from Frances, who always
gave a good account of you, I presume my
correspondent was mistaken. I this day
entered my seventy-seventh year, in as good
health and spirits, thank God, as I have
done on any one birthday for the last half
century. I am moving about upon my farm
from eight o'clock in the morning till four
in the afternoon, without suffering the least
from fatigue. I sent in my claim to the
Board of Agriculture for their premium for
a cure for the mildew on wheat, but do not
yet know whether it is admitted. I do not

know whether I ever mentioned to you a machine for dibbling or planting wheat, which I have brought to great perfection. I have a very material improvement on the stocks, respecting ploughs and wheel carriages, but of this I shall say nothing till I have brought it to the proof, which I hope to be able to do very shortly, when you shall be immediately apprized of the result, whether favourable or not.

" Have you seen Lord John Russell's letter to Lord Holland; and what do you, and other judges, think of it? The first time you go by Harding's, No. 36, St. James'-street, I shall thank you to desire he will send me ' Ratcliff's Survey of Flanders,' as soon as published.

" I am, dear Brother,

" Affectionately yours,

" EDMUND CARTWRIGHT."

"TO DR. PEARSON.

" Sept. 4th, 1820.

" MY DEAR SIR,—Though the complaint which I mentioned in my last is happily removed, I have had a return of the bile, as you will see by the following epigram :—

"EQUAL JUSTICE.

" If such criminal acts have her conduct pervaded
As are charged on the Queen, let her e'en be degraded;
Yet this will I say—neither treason nor slander—
What is sauce for the goose should be sauce for the gander.

The remainder of my letter I shall devote to something more important than epigrams or Attic salt, should they contain any. You may recollect the experiment that I made two years ago with salt, as a remedy for the mildew on wheat.* I have this year

* See "Philosophical Magazine," vol. lvi., p. 395.

repeated it with the most unequivocal success, and this in one instance under circumstances which probably may never
recur. Last year I discovered a few ears
of wheat which appeared to be a new and
improved variety. These I saved; and by
dibbling them in, grain by grain, they extended over a bed four feet wide and nearly
one hundred yards long. Wishing to force
as good a crop as possible, the ground was
previously manured very highly; and in
Spring, it was dressed over more than once
with a thick coat of soot. The consequence
was, it grew as luxuriously as you may have
observed wheat that has accidentally grown
on a dunghill, and which is always mildewed
in the extreme, so as to rot on the ground
without bringing a single grain to maturity.
As soon as I perceived the mildew, which
was at a much earlier period than it usually

appears, for the straw was quite in a green state, I dressed it with salt and water, which immediately checked the disease. Fearing, however, that it might be too malignant for a single dressing, the remedy was repeated. I am happy to say the crop is completely saved, and I have no doubt will produce as marketable corn as the rest of the field. As I look upon this discovery as most highly important, I wish to give it all possible publicity. If you think the Royal Society would give attention to the subject, though it does not fall within the general scope of the matters discussed by that body at the present day, I will furnish you with a more detailed account of the business, and of the process by which the remedy is applied. Since the reduction of the duty on salt for agricultural purposes, the expense is a mere nothing."

"Oct. 21st, 1820.

"It is a received opinion, I am told, that Sir Humphry Davy will be the new President of the Royal Society. Should that be the case, I should feel an ambition to become one of its members, which I should not do, were the person placed at the head of it elevated to the situation chiefly from his rank. Will you instruct me how I am to proceed in offering myself a candidate? I must be proposed, I presume, by two or three of the members. Were I to choose who should propose me, it should be Sir Humphry Davy, Mr. Davies Gilbert, and yourself. My title to offer myself as a candidate is founded on my discovery of the remedy for the mildew on wheat, without exception one of the most important discoveries of modern times, and in a pecuniary view, as it respects the country at large, without comparison the most important. Had this discovery fortunately been known and acted upon in the years 1795 and 1800 (emphatically called the years of scarcity), the distresses of those years would probably never have been heard of."

In the latter end of the year 1820, Dr. Cartwright had the satisfaction of receiving the following interesting letters from Sir Stamford Raffles :—

"TO THE REV. EDMUND CARTWRIGHT, D.D.

"Fort Marlbro', 8th April, 1820.

" DEAR SIR,—It was only on my return from Bencoolen, that I had the pleasure to receive your letter of the 2nd February, 1819 ; and I lose no time in assuring you, that it will afford me infinite pleasure to

meet your wishes, and contribute all that
lies in my power to the success of your views
and speculations. In the present state of
Sumatra, of which so large a portion still
remains in a state of nature, there is a far
wider field for the naturalist than the horti-
culturist; and I could with greater ease
send you twenty new and undescribed plants,
than a pint of any well-known seed. I will,
however, do my best, and send you by every
opportunity a small parcel of those most
likely to interest you. The present opportunity was not foreseen, and the ship only
remains a few hours, therefore you must be
content with my present communication, as
an earnest or indication of what may come
hereafter.

" So little seems to be known in Europe
respecting the culture of dry rice, and as it
is not impossible this important grain may

be introduced into the British Isles, I take the liberty of sending you a small quantity for seed. It is grown on the hills, and generally on lands recently cleared from primitive forest; the ground is not ploughed, but on the approach of the rainy season small holes are made with a stick, and two grains of seed thrown in; the rice is then left to itself, until reaped. It is the principal cultivation of Sumatra, particularly in the mountains, where the soil is richer and the climate colder than below. The soil is generally enriched by the ashes of the newly-cleared forest burnt on the spot. I also send you a specimen of the rice: it is considered full twenty per cent. better than the lowland, or irrigated rice, and bears a proportionate high price; it is far more nutritious, and less likely to perish.

" Of wheat, barley, or oats, we have

N

none; nor am I aware of any grasses which are cultivated by seed. In these rich and luxuriant countries we find more trouble in restraining and checking nature, than in nursing and improving the gifts which she spontaneously presents to us. I will, however, endeavour, at some future period, to collect the seeds of the grasses we most esteem.

" Of vetches and oil-giving plants we have an extensive variety; few of them have yet been cultivated in England; the French bean may be an exception.

" I have taken measures for sending you, from the upper provinces of Bengal, collections of wheat, oats, peas, &c.; and though these may be long in coming to hand, they will, I hope, be acceptable. I shall also request a friend of mine at the Cape to send you, by the present opportunity, whatever is likely to interest you from thence. I am aware you have already received supplies from that quarter through Lord Charles Somerset, but duplicates will, no doubt, be useful, and there may be yet many plants there which you would desire to have.

"I am here amid groves of nutmegs, cloves, cassia, benzoin, camphor, &c.; and if any of these exotics are likely to prove interesting, pray say so.

"I beg you to accept my best acknowledgments for your highly flattering, but no less acceptable notice of my exertions in repelling Dutch aggression. Our government certainly made a sad mistake in giving up Java at all.

"Next to Great Britain, Java is, without exception, the finest island in the world —almost a fairy land. All we can do now is to prevent the Dutch from going even beyond what was intended to be restored by that convention; fortunately, they evinced their disposition and greediness too soon, and we may be able to save something out of the wreck. You will, no doubt, have heard of my new establishment at Singapore, emphatically called by the natives, the Poosab, or navel of the Malay countries; it secures all our commercial interests at little or no expense; and I am happy to say, that this decisive measure has had its full effect in checking our rivals. They have been driven out of Palembang and Rhio, and the island of Banca is nearly independent of their authority. Their establishments on Borneo are in a precarious state, and if our ministers do not make a second blunder at home they will soon be confined within their proper limits, Java and the Moluccas.

" I shall take an early opportunity of writing to you respecting your plan for bank notes. The subject requires some attention, and I have not a moment to spare at present. The present opportunity of writing direct is by the ship ' Borneo,' the first and only ship built on the island so called. She was constructed during my administration in Java, and I once hoped she might have excited the attention of our government, and induced the English to patronize and protect that important country. She is 450 tons burthen, and was built some miles inland, in the forest where the timbers were supplied. The commander, Captain Ross, no builder by profession, and without scientific or European assistance, raised her from the stocks. As long as she floats and bears her present name, she will, I think,

remind us of what we have lost, if not of
our folly in losing it.

> " I remain, my dear Sir,
>> " Yours faithfully,
>>> " T. S. RAFFLES."

" TO DR. CARTWRIGHT.

> " Bencoolen, 12th April, 1820.

" MY DEAR SIR,—I will now reply to that
part of your letter respecting the means
which this country may afford in aid of
your plan for preventing forgery on the
Bank.   The idea appears to me a good one,
and capable of easy application.   In Java
we have a very excellent material for paper
in the Morus papyrifera; but as the plant is
extensively cultivated, and that colony is
now in other hands, we could not answer for
the quantity that might be introduced into
Europe.   The same objection may, perhaps,

apply to the various materials used for the purpose in China; but the plant recently discovered in Nepaul, and described by my friend, Dr. Wallich, may, I think, answer the purpose well. The enclosed paper contains Dr. Wallich's observations on the plant, and the valuable material it furnishes for paper. Being a native of the highest regions of India, and not yet generally cultivated, it would be an easy matter for the East India Company to monopolize the whole of the produce, and to prevent the material from falling into other hands than that of the Bank. The paper which is made from this material is remarkable for its toughness; and that you may judge of its superiority in this respect, I enclose an engraving of the flower on the paper itself. It is intended, with the accompanying description by Dr. Wallich, for publication in

the next number of the ' Asiatic Researches,'
but its receipt by you may be interesting.*
I understand Dr. Wallich had it in contemplation to send a quantity of the paper, as
well as of the material for making it, home
to the Court of Directors, and if you apply
at the India House, you may possibly obtain
further information on the subject.

" Yours, very truly,

" T. S. RAFFLES."

---

* Lord Amherst, on going out to India about
three years afterwards, kindly undertook to procure
some of the seeds of this plant for Dr. Cartwright,
who was desirous to ascertain, by experiment, whether a plant which flourishes in those parts of Nepaul
where snow lies, and where oaks are produced, might
grow well in our own country. Dr. Cartwright had
requested that the seeds might be packed in raw
sugar, as the best means of preserving their vegeta-
tive quality; and this method appears to be of tried
efficacy. The plant in question is a Daphne, closely
allied to D. cannabina of Loureira.

CHAPTER IX.

DR. BARDSLEY'S zealous and friendly exertions in behalf of Dr. Cartwright's claims to parliamentary remuneration have been already mentioned. It will not, therefore, be matter of surprise, that one whose heart was so warm and generous should not only feel the obligation, but delight to own it; for Dr. Cartwright, though very apt to forget the favours he bestowed on others, could never forget those which he had received himself.

In a letter addressed to this gentleman on the 20th Nov. 1820, Dr. Cartwright says, " The world is more your debtor than you are aware of; the leisure and independence, for which I was mainly indebted to your friendship, will enable me, as I hope, to benefit the public to an extent which I could never have foreseen." He then mentions his experiments in the application of human power, and proceeds to inform his correspondent of his success in using salt and water as a remedy for mildew. " There are two methods," says he, "in applying it.* Two men to spread the mixture, and one to supply them with it, will get over four acres

---

* Objections have been made to the difficulty of this operation; but those who have witnessed the easy method of distributing liquid manure over the fields in Germany and Switzerland, will not, perhaps, be inclined to raise this objection.

in a day; six or eight bushels of salt are sufficient for an acre, the expense of which is trifling at the price for which it can be procured for farming purposes. It is paid for in the improvement of the manure made from the salted straw. The mildew on wheat is ascertained to be a parasitical plant, of the fungus kind. The principal constituent in the composition of fungi being water (witness the manufactory of mushroom catsup), when brought in contact with the salt, their aqueous particles are absorbed by the salt, and the fungi immediately die. Salt has no effect upon the wheat at the time the mildew is upon it, as the straw is then fibrous, and on fibre, whether vegetable or animal, salt acts rather as a preservative than otherwise."

In 1819, Dr. C. had communicated to the " Philosophical Magazine," (vol. liii.

p. 425,) an account of a locomotive carriage which he had constructed, to be worked by human power. On the axle of the driving wheels were two cranks, connected with treadles, worked by each foot of the driver alternately. By means of shoulder-straps affixed to the carriage, the operator could, when necessary, apply a considerable muscular force, in addition to his absolute weight, to the propulsion of the vehicle. During the three following years, Dr. Cartwright employed this carriage for the conveyance of necessaries from the neighbouring market towns, and, occasionally, even from London. Indeed, it would appear, from the following letter, that he had brought it to a considerable degree of perfection.

"TO DR. BARDSLEY.

"April 24th, 1822.

"This is a memorable day with me, and I therefore dedicate part of it to you, to whose friendship my latter years are indebted for a considerable share of their comfort and independence.

"On this day I enter my eightieth year. This, however, I do, in common with thousands; but what makes it particularly memorable is, that on this day I have completed my invention of a carriage to go without horses, which I call a centaur carriage. Two men took a cart from my house (the cart and its load weighing sixteen cwt.), a distance of twenty-seven miles in a day, and up two very long and steep hills. Since then I have greatly improved upon it. It is now so constructed, that I can give it what speed I please. Its greatest advantage, I am of opinion—for I have not yet had the opportunity of absolutely ascertaining it—will be in going fast; for the exertion of the men is the same, whether the carriage goes fast or slow, its speed depending on its internal mechanism. This carriage will be particularly useful in mercantile situations.

" My youngest daughter is a good lithographist, and when I go to town I will get her to make some drawings of the carriage, to explain its mechanism, a copy of which I will send you, and which you may put into Joe Taylor's hands; it may possibly be of use to him.

" Some little time ago, when I was labouring at this business, the following lines occurred to me, by which you will see that, though the powers of body and mind may be giving way, my perseverance is not materially abated :—

" Since even Newton owns, that all he wrought
' Was due to industry and patient thought;'
What shall restrain the impulse that I feel
To forward, as I may, the public weal;
By his example fired, to break away,
In quest of truth, through darkness into day?
He tried, on venturous wing, the loftiest flight—
An eagle soaring to the fount of light;
I cleave to earth, to earth-born arts confined,
A worm of science of the humblest kind !
Our powers, though wide apart as earth and heaven,
For different purposes alike were given;
Though mine the arena of inglorious fame,
Where pride and folly would the strife disclaim,
With mind unwearied, still will I engage,
In spite of failing vigour and of age,
Nor quit the conflict till I quit the stage;
Or if in idleness my life shall close,
May well-earned victory justify repose.

"Have you heard anything of a new Royal Society, instituted by the King, to which he gives, or has promised to give, annually,

1000*l.* It is called the Royal Society of
Literature. I am a member of it; our
president is the Bishop of St. David's.
There are premiums given of one hundred
guineas for the best poem, one for the best
dissertation on the Greek language, and
another for the best dissertation on the
character of Homer.   Seventeen candidates,
I hear, have started for the two others.
The poetical premium was last year awarded
to Mrs. Hemans; the subject, in every sense,
I should have thought a barren one; but
her poem, I am told—for it has not yet
reached me—is very beautiful.   In your
next letter you will, I hope, give a better
account of yourself than you did in your
last.   It will give you pleasure to hear that
it has pleased God to continue to me the
same good health that I have enjoyed for
years past, with little or no sensible abate-

ment. Mrs. C. sends her kindest remem-
brances, and I am, dear sir,

"Most faithfully yours,

"EDMUND CARTWRIGHT."

In September, 1822, Dr. Cartwright
visited Dover, and writing from thence to
Dr. Bardsley, he says, "I am not a little
gratified by the partial view you take of
my endeavours to make myself useful to
the world so long as it shall please God
to continue me in it. I came here for the
benefit of warm sea-bathing, having been
much unhinged by the hot weather in August. I have only bathed twice, and am
now as stout again as ever. In a conversation I had with the bath man, I learned
that to fill his cistern in a given time was
full work for two athletic men; I told him
of my principle of exerting human power,

and that if he would furnish me with a workman, I would shew him how to apply it to his pump. In the course of a day the work was finished, and now an active lad will do the business in half the usual time, and, comparatively speaking, with very little fatigue. If the success of this experiment should lead to the building of a vessel to be navigated upon the same principle, you will have the opportunity of going next year to Calais without the risk of fire or explosion, or the danger of being sunk or overset; for if the vessel is constructed as I propose, to sink or overset it will be, morally speaking, impossible. Mrs. Cartwright and I are delighted with the prospect of shewing you what a comfortable spot your kindness has contributed to place us in. It will not be more than twenty miles out of the direct road from London to Dover, and I am willing to believe you will find the air of Hollanden of great benefit to Mrs. Bardsley and yourself; of its salubrity, as far as I am concerned, I can speak in the highest terms, and I do not think, considering the delicate state of health Mrs. Cartwright has been in for some years, that she could have been better anywhere else. The other friend to whom I feel indebted, jointly with yourself, for the ease and comfort of my present existence, was Hawkins Browne, whose weight and influence carried the business of which you laid the foundation stone through the House of Commons. A posthumous work of his has lately been published, entitled 'Essays, &c.,' printed for Cadell. I sent for it, merely for the purpose of keeping it as a memorial of a dear and valued friend. To my most agreeable surprise, I found it a work of superlative merit. If you have not seen it, I would recommend it to your perusal. It is the best connected chain of reasoning on the subject of morals and religion I ever met with.

"A few weeks ago I sent in a paper to the Royal Society, of which I am a member. It has been read, and, I hear, been complimented on its profundity and acuteness; but as it is considered purely theoretical, it is not admissible into their transactions, which are confined to absolute facts, or truths that can be substantiated by mathematical demonstration, which mine certainly cannot, at least by me.

"It is a new theory of the planetary system, as far as relates to the power by which the planets are impelled round the sun. As soon as I get home, I will send you a copy of the paper. You will, I hope, make all due allowance for it, as being an initiatory

treatise of a young philosopher just com-
mencing his philosophical studies and career.*

"A steam vessel arrived this morning from
Ramsgate on a party of pleasure, the passengers above 300. They returned after
an early dinner. Just as they were ready
to set off, two others arrived from France:
they had all bands of music on board. The
day was uncommonly fine, the pier crowded
by spectators; it was a most splendid sight,
and I must own I felt no little gratification
in reflecting on the share I had in contributing to the exhibition. You probably
do not know that Fulton, who first brought
steam navigation forward, was a most intimate friend of mine, and of course I lent
him all the assistance in my power, of which

* In January, 1823, Dr. Cartwright received the
thanks of the Literary and Philosophical Society of
Manchester, for a paper on this subject, which was
read before the society.

I believe there is one proof still in existence—I mean, a model, to shew how the power of steam might be applied. When I went to Woburn, I gave it to Lord John Russell, then about ten or eleven years old, as a plaything: it went by clock-work. His lordship used frequently to amuse himself with setting it afloat on the stew-ponds in the garden. If it is not worn out, his younger brothers may possibly amuse themselves with it to this day."

"TO DR. BARDSLEY.

"24th April, 1823.

" MY DEAR SIR,—I have this year completed my eightieth year. In looking back upon the events of my past life, and making a fair estimate of its joys and sorrows, it would be ungrateful to the Author of all good, not to acknowledge that the good has greatly overbalanced the evil; neither can I forget for how much of that good I have been, and still am, indebted to your exertions. If you should feel induced to become a member of our new society, entitled the Royal Society of Literature, I should be proud to propose you. It does not, however, appear clearly, to me at least, what good it will do. Literature in the present day wants no stimulus; I rather incline to the opinion that another Caliph Omar is more wanting, to burn nine-tenths of the books we already have.

"I lately amused myself in drawing up what may be called a bird's-eye view of literature, taking my documents from the 'Dictionary of Living Authors,' from which it appears that at the time it was compiled (1816), there were between five and six thousand authors then in existence, and that the family of living poets, of which I have been for these twenty years the father, consisted of no fewer than 704!"

Hitherto the subject of these memoirs had enjoyed, as he himself gratefully acknowledges in the preceding letter to Dr. Bardsley, an extraordinary exemption from the usual infirmities of age. To this exemption, it is probable that early rising, and the temperate habits of his life, had mainly contributed. His fine intellectual countenance still beamed with undiminished intelligence; his benevolent and placid character retained all its natural cheerfulness; while his firm step and healthful complexion seemed to promise many years of prolonged usefulness and activity.

But we are now approaching the period when his robust constitution began to shew symptoms of increasing weakness, and notwithstanding the watchful attention and solicitude which Mrs. Cartwright bestowed on his declining health, it was evident that the failure was rapid, and that no human power could arrest its progress.

Surely, in this case, the sudden transition may be considered as a merciful dispensation, when we compare it with those instances in which imbecility, fretfulness, and suffering accompany a lengthened existence, and when, as the great moralist expresses it,

" Superfluous lags the veteran on the stage."*

Not so our veteran mechanic, who in July 1823, within three months of his lamented death, writes thus to Dr. Pearson:—

" MY DEAR SIR,—Since I wrote last to you, I have luckily discovered a method of working an engine by explosion, in a

* See " Johnson's Vanity of Human Wishes."

way to be perfectly secure from danger,
and completely effectual. You will be surprised when I tell you it is by gunpowder.
To give continuous action to that which
is instantaneous—or, in other words, to control the velocity of such an exploding body
as gunpowder, so as to produce steady and
equable movement, *hic labor hoc opus.*
This, my dear sir, I have (in theory) accomplished; and by a contrivance, equally
certain as it is simple—more simple, indeed,
than the lock of a common gun. As soon
as a model of it is made (which, though it
will not be one hour's work, I may probably
not get these three days) you shall know
the result. Were gunpowder a dearer article
than it is, yet as the heavy expense of fuel
would be saved, my mode of working an
engine may possibly be as cheap, power for

power, as steam. The weight of the engine, an object for my purpose of great importance, as well as the prime cost, and the space it would occupy, would not, I apprehend, be more than one fourth of Perkins's. In my engine there will be this advantage— its power may be increased or diminished at pleasure, merely by regulating the feed of powder; and as the stress upon the engine will lie in a small compass, that particular part might be made to sustain any pressure without inconvenience, and without any additional load of metal worth speaking of. Should my ideas on this business be, as I have every reason to think, correct, the discovery will be one of the greatest importance. I had a vast deal more to have written to you about, one thing or other, but in truth I am downright tired, and I

must walk out for a little fresh air into my
hay-field."

In another letter to Dr. Pearson, written
about this time, Dr. Cartwright thus pur-
sues the subject. "You are aware," says
he, "that if a sufficient quantity of gunpowder to make a complete stroke of the
piston were to be fired off at once, the
explosion would not only be highly dangerous, but, from its instantaneous effect,
equally useless. Now, by giving a subdued
and continuous action, the engine would be
perfectly under command, and its action
steady and equable. I will endeavour to
explain how this is produced. Supposing
it would require sixty grains of powder to
make a comple stroke of the piston, instead
of firing off the whole at once, it is to be
delivered by a contrivance something like
the drill-box of a sowing machine, only, we

will say, three grains at a time, and at equal intervals, so that each individual explosion would be but the one-twentieth part of the whole. Supposing, therefore, the stroke of the piston and its return to occupy two seconds of time, there would be ten minor explosions in a second, which, though individually feeble, compared with the mass of powder, yet the aggregate expansion and force would be the same; but by being subdivided, and the explosions following in succession, the action of the engine would be uniform and steady. In addition to what I have said above, I will further observe, that the engine will be so constructed as to make it next to impossible that the powder should explode improperly; and even if it should, it will be so contrived, that such an accident, supposing it to happen, will be attended with no danger. I intend to call my engine, *par excellence*, the safety machine. You know very well, my dear sir, that some of the most deadly poisons, if administered judiciously, and in small doses, become remedies both safe and judicious. I am only applying those principles and practices to mechanical bodies which you have so often successfully applied to bodies that are animated."

"TO DR. BARDSLEY.

"September 8th, 1823.

"MY DEAR SIR,—I was glad to see by the Manchester paper, which came to my hand a few days ago, that you had withdrawn yourself from part of your professional labours, which I hoped might be a prelude to your withdrawing yourself altogether from the whole of them, and that we shall shortly see you in the south. My friend

Taylor, I observe, has lately taken out a patent. Most sincerely do I wish the worthy old man may benefit himself by it. I am not quite certain that I may not follow his example,* having made a discovery of substituting gunpowder, in the place of steam, for working engines. The

* Notwithstanding this intention, Dr. Cartwright's opinion does not seem to have been favourable to the protection afforded by patent rights. This opinion, which was unfortunately derived from his own experience, is thus humorously expressed in a former letter to Dr. Bardsley, in September, 1822:—" A patent is a feeble protection against the rapacity, piracy, and theft of too many of the manufacturing class. There is scarcely an instance, I believe, of a patent being granted for any invention of real value, against which attempts have not been made to overthrow or evade it. It might be supposed that whatever was confessedly original, and which had never been heard or thought of before, would have some chance to escape the attacks of the invader. No such thing. Were that eminent sur

whole contrivance is simplicity itself.   I
was afraid, a few days ago, that old age was
rapidly advancing upon me, as for the space
of forty-eight hours I felt uncommonly weak
and debilitated. I thank God, those feelings
have entirely left me."

A return of these symptoms induced Dr.

geon and anatomist, Mr. Carpue, who, it is said, has
lately furnished some of his patients with supple-
mental noses, to discover a method of putting an
additional pair of eyes into a man's head, and to take
out a patent for the discovery, I should not be surprised if forty witnesses were to come forward to
swear that it was not a new invention, 'for that they
had seen forty people, with forty extra pair of eyes in
their heads, forty years ago.'   Far be it from me to
insinuate that forty pair of lawyers could be found
who would try to persuade a jury to give credit to
such evidence.   As there are, however, many very
honourable men among the great body of manufacturers, several indeed within my own knowledge,
whom I would wish to benefit, I recommend this
discovery to their notice."

Cartwright to try the effect of change of air and warm bathing. He accordingly removed to Hastings, on the 8th of October, 1823; but he no longer derived the same benefit which he had experienced from his excursion to Dover in the preceding year.

Yet though the powers of life were thus rapidly sinking, his mind was as strong as ever; and it was afterwards remarked by his nephew, the Rev. Henry Hodges, that. while occasionally sitting with his uncle on the beach at Hastings, he was equally charmed by the vigour and cheerfulness of his conversation, and could scarcely bring himself to believe that the hour was at hand, when that harmonious voice would be mute for ever.

Aware of his own precarious state, Dr. Cartwright bore his illness with that sweetness and submission which might have been expected from the character which we have been endeavouring thus faintly to delineate, and humbly resigning himself to the will of his God and Saviour, he expired on the 30th of October, 1823. His remains were interred in the church at Battle, in Sussex.*

---

* Of Dr. Cartwright's children, (all of whom were by his first wife,) the following survived him—viz., 1, Edmund Cartwright, M.A., F.S.A., Rector of Earnley, author of the "Topographical History of the Rape of Bramber, in Western Sussex," deceased in 1833; 2, Mary, the wife of Henry Eustatius Strickland, Esq.; 3, Elizabeth, wife of the Rev. John Penrose, well known under the name of "Mrs. Markham," as the author of several popular works for young persons—viz., Histories of England, France, Poland, &c., deceased in 1837; and, 4, Frances Dorothy, author of the "Life and Correspondence of Major Cartwright."

His eldest brother, Captain George Cartwright, was a man of strong and original cast of mind. A

Several brief notices of Dr. Cartwright have already appeared in print—viz., in the Annual Obituary for 1823, in the Gentleman's Magazine for December in the same year, in the Monthly Magazine for January, 1824, in the Dictionnaire des Contemporains, and in the Algemeine Deutsche Real En-

journal which he kept during a residence of many years on the coast of Labrador, was published in three volumes, 4to, in 1792. It is written in a pure and manly style, and gives a curious picture of the hardships, voluntary on his part, of a hunter's life, relieved by very interesting anecdotes of those inoffensive and unsophisticated people, the Esquimaux.

Of his much attached brother John, well known as Major Cartwright, we will merely observe, that the same purity and disinterestedness influenced his private life that had guided his public conduct. In his own family, from youth to age, he had been the steadiest of friends and most affectionate of brothers.

cyclopädie, or Conversations Lexicon, published in 1827.* A short account of Dr. Cartwright has also been published in a volume of the Library of Entertaining Knowledge, as well as another notice in the Gallery of British Portraits. There is a brief account of his discovery of the power-loom in two articles in the Edinburgh Review for June, 1827, and October, 1833, and also a sketch of his life in the Penny Cyclopædia.

The following letter was written soon after Dr. Cartwright's death, by Dr. Bardsley, to Samuel Oldknow, Esq., but the suggestion it contained was not carried into effect :—

* While travelling in Switzerland, in June, 1838, one of Dr. Cartwright's daughters had the pleasure of finding at Berne, a short, but correct biography of her father in the Pfennig Encyclopädie, published at Leipzig, by C. E. Kollman.

Nov. 25, 1823.

"DEAR SIR,—It is probable you will have been informed by the public papers of the rather sudden death of my excellent friend, Dr. Cartwright. His varied talents, his general acquirements, his inventive genius, his gentleness and humility, have scarcely ever been surpassed. Such a man should not go down to the grave without a public memorial of his worth! I find it is the intention of his London friends to erect a monument by subscription, setting forth his various and useful discoveries, and his constant endeavours to benefit mankind during a long and active life. Messrs. Smith, the bankers, in London, have warmly entered into this plan; and it is wished by them that the names of some of the leading commercial men of Manchester should grace the list. Those gentlemen who kindly petitioned parliament for a remuneration for his inventions and improvements, especially in regard to the power-loom, might have no objection to promote the erection of such a monument to departed genius. If this proposal meet with your approbation, perhaps you will do me the favour to acquaint me with your intentions, and lend your assistance to augment the subscription in your town and neighbourhood.

"I remain, dear Sir,

"Yours, very respectfully,

"S. A. BARDSLEY.

"It is intended that the Manchester gentlemen should head the list."

With this appropriate testimony of respect to Dr. Cartwright's memory—a testimony as creditable to the venerable writer, whose zeal thus extended beyond the grave, as it is just to the object of his unwearied friendship, we close this brief and, we fear, imperfect memoir of one of the most ingenious and amiable of men.

In a case where natural partiality may be supposed to bias the judgment of the writer, it seems almost presumptuous to guide that of the reader; and yet we hope we may be pardoned for pointing out, that what appears particularly worthy of admiration in the character of Dr. Cartwright, and which ought to be held out as deserving of imitation, is that generous self-devotion, that constant benevolence of purpose, which, from youth to age, never lost sight of the smallest available opportunity of promoting the benefit of others.

APPENDIX.

A.

ARMINE AND ELVIRA: A LEGENDARY TALE.

(See p. 17.)

THE preceding Memoir has been chiefly devoted to the history of Dr. Cartwright's mechanical and scientific labours. But as some of our readers may wish to be further informed as to his poetical powers, we have been induced to republish one of his early productions, which, though enjoying great popularity in its day, has been long out of print. The reader will perceive that it belongs to the refined and classic school of the last century, before poets had ventured on those brilliant but eccentric flights which attract so much favour at the present day.

PART I.

A hermit on the banks of Trent,
    Far from the world's bewildering maze,
To humbler scenes of calm content
    Had fled from brighter, busier days.

If haply from his guarded breast
    Should steal the unsuspected sigh,
And memory, an unbidden guest,
    With former passions fill'd his eye;

Then pious Hope and Duty praised
   The wisdom of th' Unerring Sway;
And while his eye to heaven he raised,
   Its silent waters stole away.

Life's gayer ensigns once he bore—
   Ah! what avails the mournful tale?
Suffice it, when the scene was o'er,
   He fled to the sequester'd vale.

" What though the joys I loved so well,
   The charms," he cried, " that youth has known,
Fly from the hermit's lonely cell!
   Yet is not Armine still my own?

" Yes, Armine, yes, thou valued youth!
   'Midst every grief thou still art mine!
Dear pledge of Winifreda's truth,
   And solace of my life's decline!

" Though from the world and worldly care
   My wearied mind I mean to free,
Yet ev'ry hour that Heav'n can spare,
   My Armine, I devote to thee.

" And sure that Heaven my hopes shall bless,
   And make thee famed for virtues fair,
And happy, too, if happiness
   Depend upon a parent's prayer.

" Last hope of life's departing day,
  In whom its future scenes I see!
No truant thought shall ever stray
  From this lone hermitage and thee."

Thus, to his humble fate resign'd,
  His breast each anxious care foregoes ;
All but the care of Armine's mind,
  The dearest task a parent knows!

And well were all his cares repaid ;
  In Armine's breast each virtue grew,
In full maturity display'd
  To fond Affection's anxious view.

Nor yet neglected were the charms,
  To polish'd life that grace impart ;
Virtue, he knew, but feebly warms,
  'Till Science humanize the heart.

And when he saw the lawless train
  Of passions in the youthful breast,
He curb'd them, not with rigid rein,
  But strove to soothe them into rest.

" Think not, my son, in this," he cried,
  " A father's precept shall displease :
No—be each passion gratified
  That tends to happiness or ease.

" Nor shall th' ungrateful task be mine
  Their native generous warmth to blame,
That warmth if Reason's suffrage join
  To point the object and the aim.

" This suffrage wanting, know, fond boy,
  That every passion proves a foe :
Though much it deal in promised joy,
  It pays, alas ! in certain woe.

" Complete Ambition's wildest scheme ;
  In Power's all-brilliant robes appear ;
Indulge in Fortune's golden dream ;
  Then ask thy breast if Peace be there :

" No : it shall tell thee, Peace retires
  If once of her loved friends deprived ;
Contentment calm, subdu'd desires,
  And happiness that's self-derived."

To temper thus the stronger fires
  Of youth he strove, for well he knew,
Boundless as thought though man's desires,
  The real wants of life were few.

And oft revolving in his breast
  Th' insatiate lust of Wealth or Fame,
He, with no common care opprest,
  To Fortune thus would oft exclaim :

" O Fortune ! at thy crowded shrine
    What wretched worlds of suppliants bow !
For ever hail'd thy pow'r divine,
    For ever breath'd the serious vow.

" With tottering pace and feeble knee,
    See Age advance in shameless haste ;
The palsied hand is stretched to thee
    For wealth he wants the power to taste.

" See, led by Hope, the youthful train,
    Her fairy dreams their hearts have won ;
She points to what they ne'er shall gain,
    Or dearly gain—to be undone.

" Must I, too, form the votive prayer,
    And wilt thou hear one suppliant more ?
His prayer, O Fortune, deign to hear,
    To thee who never pray'd before.

" O may one dear, one favour'd youth,
    May Armine still thy pow'r disclaim ;
Kneel only at the shrine of Truth,
    Count Freedom Wealth, and Virtue Fame."

Lo ! to his utmost wishes blest
    The prayer was heard ; and Freedom's flame,
And Truth, the sunshine of the breast,
    Were Armine's wealth, were Armine's fame.

His heart no selfish cares confined,
  He felt for all that feel distress,
And, still benevolent and kind,
  He blest them, or he wish'd to bless.

For what though Fortune's frown deny
  With wealth to bid the sufferer live?
Yet Pity's hand can oft supply
  A balm she never knew to give:

Can oft with lenient drops assuage
  The wounds no ruder hand can heal,
When Grief, Despair, Distraction, rage,
  While Death the lips of Love shall seal.

Ah! then, his anguish to remove,
  Deprived of all his heart holds dear,
How sweet the still surviving love
  Of Friendship's smile, of Pity's tear!

This knew the sire: he oft would cry —
  " From these, my son, O ne'er depart!
These tender charities, that tie
  In mutual league the human heart.

" Be thine those feelings of the mind
  That wake at honour's, friendship's call;
Benevolence, that unconfined
  Extends her liberal hand to all.

" By Sympathy's untutor'd voice
 Be taught her social laws to keep ;
Rejoice with them that do rejoice,
 And weep with them that weep.

" The heart that bleeds for others' woes,
 Shall feel each selfish sorrow less ;
His breast who happiness bestows,
 Reflected happiness shall bless.

" Each ruder passion still withstood
 That breaks o'er Virtue's sober line,
The tender, noble, and the good,
 To cherish and indulge be thine.

" And yet, my Armine, might I name
 One passion as a dangerous guest ?
Well may'st thou wonder when I blame
 The tenderest, noblest, and the best.

" Nature, 'tis true, with Love design'd
 To smoothe the race our fathers ran,
The savage of the human kind
 By Love was soften'd into man.

" As feels the ore the searching fire,
 Expanding and refining too,
So fairer glow'd each fair desire,
 Each gentle thought so gentler grew.

" How changed, alas! those happier days!
  A train how different now succeeds!
While sordid Avarice betrays,
  Or empty Vanity misleads.

" Fled from the heart each nobler guest,
  Each genuine feeling we forego;
What Nature planted in the breast,
  The flowers of love, are weeds of woe.

" Hence all the pangs the heart must feel
  Between contending passions toss'd,
Wild Jealousy's avenging steel,
  And life and fame and virtue lost!

" Yet falling life, yet fading fame,
  Compared to what his heart annoy
Who cherishes a hopeless flame,
  Are terms of happiness and joy.

" Ah! then, the soft contagion fly!
  And timely shun th' alluring bait!"
The rising blush, the downcast eye,
  Proclaim'd—The Precept was too late.

PART II.

Deep in the bosom of a wood,
　　Where Art had form'd the moated isle,
An antique castle towering stood;
　　In Gothic grandeur rose the pile.

Here Raymond, long in arms renown'd,
　　From scenes of war would oft repair;
His bed an only daughter crown'd,
　　And smiled away a father's care.

By Nature's happiest pencil drawn,
　　She wore the vernal morning's ray:
The vernal morning's blushing dawn
　　Breaks not so beauteous into day.

Her breast, impatient of control,
　　Scorn'd in its silken chains to lie,
And the soft language of the soul
　　Flow'd from her never silent eye.

The bloom that open'd on her face
　　Well seem'd an emblem of her mind,
Where snowy innocence we trace,
　　With blushing modesty combined.

P

To these resistless grace impart
　　That look of sweetness form'd to please,
That elegance, devoid of art,
　　That dignity that's lost in ease.

What youth so cold could view unmoved
　　The maid that every beauty shared?
Her Armine saw—he saw, he loved,
　　He loved—alas! and he despair'd!

Unhappy youth! he sunk oppress'd;
　　For much he labour'd to conceal
That gentlest passion of the breast,
　　Which *all* can feign, but *few* can feel.

Ingenuous fears suppress'd the flame,
　　Yet still he own'd its hidden power;
With transport dwelling on her name,
　　He soothed the solitary hour.

" How long," he cried, " must I conceal
　　What yet my heart could wish were known?
How long the truest passion feel,
　　And yet that passion fear to own?

" Ah! might I breathe my humble vow!
　　Might she, too, deign to lend an ear!
Elvira's self should then allow
　　That Armine was at least sincere.

" Wild wish! to deem the matchless maid
   Would listen to a youth like me,
Or that my vows could e'er persuade,
   Sincere and constant though they be!

" Ah! what avails my love or truth?
   She listens to no lowly swain;
Her charms must bless some happier youth,
   Some youth of Fortune's titled train.

" Then go, fallacious Hope! adieu!
   The flattering prospect I resign;
And bear from my deluded view
   The bliss that never must be mine!

" Yet will the youth, whoe'er he be,
   In truth or tenderness excel?
Or will he on thy charms, like me,
   With fondness never dying dwell?

" Will he with thine his hopes unite?
   With ready zeal thy joys improve?
With fond attention and delight
   Each wish prevent, each fear remove?

" Will he, still faithful to thy charms,
   For constant love be long rever'd?
Nor quit that heaven within thy arms
   By every tender tie endear'd?

" What though his boastful heart be vain
  Of all that birth or fortune gave?
Yet is not mine, though rude and plain,
  At least as noble and as brave?

" Then be its gentle suit preferr'd!
  Its tender sighs, Elvira, hear!
In vain—I sigh, but sigh unheard;
  Unpitied falls this lonely tear!"

Twice twelve revolving moons had past,
  Since first he caught the fatal view;
Unchanged by time his sorrows last,
  Uncheer'd by hope his passion grew.

That passion to indulge, he sought
  In Raymond's groves the deepest shade;
There Fancy's haunting spirit brought
  The image of his long-loved maid.

But hark! what more than mortal sound
  Steals on Attention's raptured ear!
The voice of Harmony around
  Swells in wild whispers soft and clear.

Can human hand a tone so fine
  Sweep from the string with touch profane?
Can human lip, with breath divine,
  Pour on the gale so sweet a strain?

'Tis she—the source of Armine's woe!
  'Tis she—whence all his joy must spring!
From her loved lips the numbers flow,
  Her magic hand awakes the string.

Now, Armine, now, thy love proclaim—
  Thy instant suit the time demands;
Delay not! Tumult shakes his frame,
  And lost in ecstasy he stands!

What magic chains thee to the ground?
  What star malignant rules the hour—
That thus, in fix'd delirium drown'd,
  Each sense intranced hath lost its power?

The trance dispel! Awake! arise!
  Speak what untutor'd love inspires!
The moment's past—thy wild surprise
  She sees, nor unalarm'd retires.

" Stay, sweet illusion, stay thy flight!
  'Tis gone! Elvira's form it wore.
Yet one more glimpse of short delight!
  'Tis gone! to be beheld no more.

" Fly, loitering feet, the charm pursue
  That plays upon my hopes and fears!
Ha! no illusion mocks my view!
  'Tis she—Elvira's self appears!

" And shall I on her steps intrude ?
  Alarm her in these lonely shades ?
O stay, fair nymph ! no ruffian rude,
  With base intent, your walk invades.

" Far gentler thoughts"—his faltering tongue,
  By humble diffidence restrain'd,
Paus'd in suspense—but thus, ere long,
  As love impell'd, its power regain'd.

" Far gentler thoughts that form inspires !
  With me, far gentler passions dwell ;
This heart hides only blameless fires,
  Yet burns with what it fears to tell.

" The faltering voice, that fears control,
  Blushes, that inward fires declare,—
Each tender tumult of the soul
  In silence owns Elvira there."

He said; and as the trembling dove,
  Sent forth t' explore the watery plain,
Soon fear'd her flight might fatal prove,
  And sudden sought her ark again—

His heart recoil'd, as one that rued
  What he too hastily confest;
And all the rising soul, subdued,
  Sought refuge in his inmost breast.

The tender strife Elvira saw,
    Distress'd; and as some parent mild,
When arm'd with words and looks of awe,
    Melts o'er the terrors of her child,

Reproof prepar'd, and angry fear,
    In soft sensations died away;
They felt the force of Armine's tear,
    And fled from pity's rising sway.

" That mournful voice, that modest air,
    Young stranger, speak the courteous breast;
Then why to these rude scenes repair,
    Of shades the solitary guest?

" And who is she whose fortunes bear
    Elvira's melancholy name?
O may those fortunes prove more fair
    Than hers who sadly owns the same."

" Ah, gentle maid! in mine survey
    A heart," he cries, " that's yours alone!
Long has it own'd Elvira's sway,
    Though long unnoticed and unknown.

" On Sherwood's old heroic plain,
    Elvira graced the festal day;
There, foremost of the youthful train,
    Her Armine bore the prize away.

" There first that form my eyes survey'd
　　With future hopes that fill'd my heart ;
But ah ! beneath that frown they fade—
　　Depart—vain, vanquish'd hopes, depart !"

He said ; and on the ground his eyes
　　Were fix'd abash'd : th' attentive maid,
Lost in the tumult of surprise,
　　The well-remember'd youth survey'd.

The transient colour went and came,
　　The struggling bosom sunk and rose ;
The trembling tumults of her frame,
　　The strong-conflicting soul disclose.

The time, the scene, she saw with dread,
　　Like Cynthia setting, glanced away ;
But scatter'd blushes as she fled—
　　Blushes that spoke a brighter day.

A friendly shepherd's neighbouring shed,
　　To pass the live-long night, he sought ;
And hope, the lover's downy bed,
　　A sweeter charm than slumber brought.

On every thought Elvira dwelt—
　　The tender air, the aspect kind,
The pity that he found she felt,
　　And all the angel in her mind.

No self-plumed vanity was there,
　　With fancied consequence elate ;
Unknown to her the haughty air
　　That means to speak superior state.

Her brow no keen resentments arm ;
　　No swell of empty pride she knew,
In trivial minds that takes th' alarm,
　　Should humble love aspire to sue.

Such love, by flattering charms betray'd,
　　Shall yet, indignant, soon rebel ;
And, blushing for the choice he made,
　　Shall fly where gentler virtues dwell.

'Tis then the mind, from bondage free,
　　And all its former weakness o'er,
Asserts its native dignity,
　　And scorns what folly prized before.

The scanty pane the rising ray
　　On the plain wall in diamonds threw,
The lover hail'd the welcome day,
　　And to his favourite scene he flew.

There soon Elvira bent her way,
　　Where long her lonely walks had been ;
Nor less had the preceding day,
　　Nor Armine less, endear'd the scene.

P 3

Oft, as she pass'd, her rising heart
   Its stronger tenderness confess'd ;
And oft she linger'd to impart
   To some safe shade her secret breast.

" How slow the heavy hours advance,"
   She cried, " since that eventful day,
When first I caught the fatal glance
   That stole me from myself away !

" Ah, youth beloved ! though low thy birth,
   The noble air, the manly grace,—
That look, that speaks superior worth,
   Can fashion, folly, fear erase ?

" Yet sure from no ignoble stem
   Thy lineage springs, though now unknown ;
The world, censorious, may condemn,—
   But, Armine, I am thine alone.

" To splendour only do we live ?
   Must pomp alone our thoughts employ ?
All, all that pomp and splendour give
   Is dearly bought with love and joy !

" But oh ! the favour'd youth appears !
   In pensive grief he seems to move !
My heart forebodes unnumber'd fears ;
   Support it Pity, Virtue, Love !

" Hither his footsteps seem to bend—
    Come, Resolution, to my aid!
My breast, what varying passions rend!
    Averse to go—to stay, afraid."

" Dear object of each fond desire
    That throbs tumultuous in my breast,
Why with averted glance retire?
    At Armine's presence why distress'd?

" What though he boast no titled name,
    No wide extent of rich domain?
Yet must he feel a fruitless flame,
    Must truth and nature plead in vain?"

" Think not," she said, " by forms betray'd,
    To humbler worth my heart is blind;
For soon shall every splendour fade,
    That beams not from the gifted mind.

" But first thy heart explore with care,
    With faith its fond emotions prove;
Lurks no unworthy passion there?
    Prompts not ambition bold to love?"

" Yes, lovely maid," the youth replies,
    " A bold ambition prompts my breast;
The tow'ring hope that love supplies,
    The wish in blessing to be bless'd.

" The meaner prospects I despise,
  That wealth, or rank, or power bestow;
Be yours the grovelling bliss ye prize,
  Ye sordid minds, that stoop so low!

" Be mine the more refined delights
  Of love, that banishes control;
When the fond heart with heart unites,
  And soul in unison with soul."

Elvira blush'd the warm reply,
  (To love a language not unknown,)
The milder glories fill'd her eye,
  And there a softer lustre shone.

The yielding smile that 's half suppress'd,
  The short, quick breath, the trembling tear,
The swell tumultuous of the breast,
  In Armine's favour all appear.

At each kind glance their souls unite,
  While love's soft sympathy imparts
The tender transport of delight
  That beats in undivided hearts.

Respectful to his lips he press'd
  Her yielded hand; in haste away
Her yielded hand she drew, distress'd,
  With looks that witness'd wild dismay.

" Ah! whence, fair Excellence, those fears?
   What terror unforeseen alarms?"
" See, where a father's frown appears!"
   She said, and sunk into his arms.

" My daughter! Heavens, it cannot be!
   And yet it must—Oh, dire disgrace!
Elvira have I lived to see
   Clasp'd in a peasant's vile embrace?

" This daring guilt let death repay!"—
   His vengeful arm the javelin threw;
With erring aim it wing'd its way,
   And far by Fate averted flew.

Elvira breathes—her pulses beat,
   Returning life illumes her eye;
Trembling a father's view to meet,
   She spies a reverend hermit nigh.

" Your wrath," she cries, " let tears assuage—
   Unheeded must Elvira pray?
O let an injured father's rage
   This hermit's sacred presence stay!

" Yet deem not, lost in guilty love,
   I plead to save my virgin fame;
My weakness, Virtue might approve,
   And smile on Nature's holy flame."

" Oh! welcome to my hopes again,
 My son!" the raptured hermit cries,
" I sought thee sorrowing on the plain,"—
 And all the father fill'd his eyes.

" Art thou," the raging Raymond said,
 " Of this audacious boy the sire?
Curse on the dart that idly sped,
 Nor bade his peasant soul expire!"

" His peasant soul!"—indignant fire
 Flash'd from the conscious father's eye,
" A gallant Earl is Armine's sire,
 And know, proud Chief, that Earl am I.

" Though here, within the hermit's cell
 I long have lived, unknown to fame;
Yet crowded camps and courts can tell—
 Thou, too, hast heard of Egbert's name!"

" Ah! Egbert! he whom tyrant rage
 Forced from his country's bleeding breast?
The patron of my orphan age,—
 My friend, my warrior, stands confess'd!

" But why?"—" The painful story spare,—
 That prostrate youth," said Egbert, " see!
His anguish asks a parent's care,—
 A parent once who pitied thee!"

Raymond, as one who, glancing round,
   Seems from some sudden trance to start,
Snatch'd the pale lovers from the ground,
   And held them, trembling, to his heart!

Joy, Gratitude, and Wonder, shed
   United tears o'er Hymen's reign,
And Nature her best triumph led,—
   For Love and Virtue join'd her train.

B.

LETTERS FROM SIR W. JONES.

(See p. 45.)

AMONGST the letters from Sir W. Jones to Dr. Cartwright, which are inserted in the Life of the former by Lord Teignmouth, there are two, of which portions only are published by his lordship. As the suppressed passages tend to throw light upon Sir William's character and opinions, they are here published entire, and distinguished by *italics*.

Friday night, 8 Sept. 1780.

DEAR SIR,—Your last favour I have this instant received, and am obliged to answer it in the greatest haste. I hope you have by this time received my letter, in which I informed you that I had declined a poll at Oxford, but was as much obliged to you and my other friends as if your kindness had been attended with the most brilliant success. I saw an advertisement also, in the paper, that Dr. Scott had declined. *I rejoice that our sentiments coincide; but, indeed, our sentiments are not much in fashion.* I have been told that the very Ode to which you are so indulgent lost me near twenty votes : this, however, I am unwilling to believe.

I am, with high respect and gratitude,

Your ever faithful servant,

W. JONES.

Lamb Buildings, Temple, 12 Nov., 1780.

DEAR SIR,—You have so fully proved the favourable opinion which you do me the honour to entertain of me, that I am persuaded you acquit me of any culpable neglect in delaying, for more than two months, to answer your very obliging letter. The truth is, that I had but just received it when I found myself obliged to leave England on very pressing business, and I have not long been returned from Paris. The hurry of preparing myself for so long a journey, at such a season, left me no time for giving you my hearty thanks, which I now most sincerely request you to accept, both for your kind letter and for the very elegant Sonnet with which you have rewarded me abundantly for my humble labours in the field of literature. I give you my word, that your letters and verses have greatly encouraged me in proceeding, as expeditiously as I am able, to send abroad my *Seven Arabian Poets;* and I propose to spend next month at Cambridge, in order to finish my little work, and to make use of a rare manuscript in the library of Trinity College. My own manuscript, which was copied for me at Aleppo, is very beautiful, but, unfortunately, not very correct. You may depend on receiving a copy as soon as it can be printed. *In these rambles into the wilds of Arabia, I soften the anguish which I feel, whenever I reflect on the melancholy times in which we live—times when many of the best men I know have actually resigned their seats in parliament, from a full conviction that no exertions whatever can preserve our free constitution, and that there is no room left in this country for honest ambition.* How happy I shall be, if I should be able to wait upon you in Leicestershire, or to see you in London; and assure you in person, that I am, with the greatest sincerity, dear sir, your much obliged

And ever faithful servant,

W. JONES.

C.

PORTION OF MR. CARTWRIGHT'S POWER-LOOM,

AS DESCRIBED IN HIS PATENT OF 1790.

(See p. 67.)

A. THE lathe, or frame which carries the reed.

B. The crank which moves the lathe, having a wheel upon its axis, which receives motion from C, a wheel on the principal axis. *a a*. The pickers. *b b*. The picker strings, passing over pulleys, at *c c*, to the springs. *d*. A hook, or radius, turning with its axis at *e*, which axis passes through the lathe, and also forms the axis of another hook, *f*, expressed by dotted lines, which rises up through the fly. The picker, as it is driven back by the shuttle, depresses the hook *i*, and consequently depresses the point of the hook, or radius, *g*; and this hook being connected with the hook *d*, by means of a wire passing from above the centre of the hook, or radius, *g*, to below the centre of the hook *d*, the point of the hook *d* is elevated or receives an oblique direction when the hook *i* is depressed, in the same manner as when the hook *f*, upon its own axis, is depressed.

k. A spring which keeps the hook *d* in a perpendicular direction, when the pickers are not driven or put back; in which case, when the lathe comes to, a lever, struck by the hook *d*, disconnects the loom from the moving power, and causes it to stop.

C. A wheel giving motion to the axis on which are the tappets for treading the shed. *m m*. Tappets for working the shuttle-springs. *n n*. The shuttle-springs.

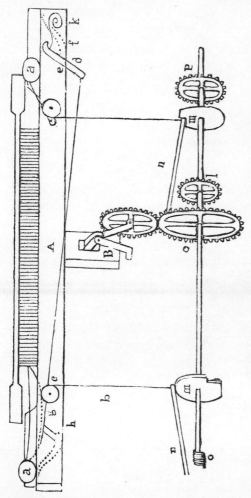

PORTION OF MR. CARTWRIGHT'S POWER-LOOM OF 1790.

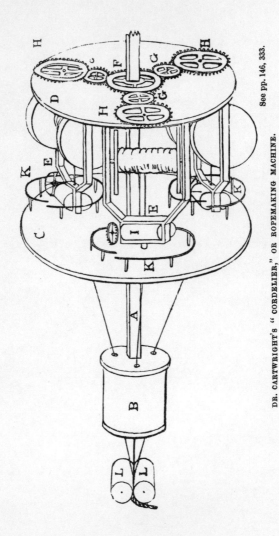

DR. CARTWRIGHT'S "CORDELIER," OR ROPEMAKING MACHINE.

See pp. 146, 333.

o. A worm or wheel for giving motion to the calender-rollers, that wind off the cloth.

p. A wheel receiving motion from a wheel of the mill.

D.

CORDELIER, OR ROPEMAKING MACHINE.
(See p. 146.)

AMONG the various mechanical contrivances which Mr. Cartwright reduced to practice in his mill at Doncaster was a machine for rope-making, to which he gave the name of the "Cordelier." This invention was thought very highly of by Mr. Fulton,—who had also turned his thoughts to the same object, as is shewn by his letters inserted pp. 141, 146. An engraving of Mr. Cartwright's Cordelier is given in the frontispiece, and is thus described in his specification of May 15, 1792.

A, the axis; B, the top, having holes through it for the strands to pass, and which serves for a gudgeon for the machine to turn upon; C, D, pulleys fixed to the axis; E E E, jacks, or spole frames; F, dead wheel within which the axis revolves; G G G, counter wheels upon the pulley D; H H H, the jack, or spole frame wheels; I I I, delivering rollers, receiving motion by means of a wheel upon the axis of one of them from K K K, hollow worms, within which they respectively revolve. The gudgeons of the jack, or spole frame next the top, are hollow, through which the strands are delivered to the top. L L, drawing rollers.

E.

MR. CARTWRIGHT'S PATENT BRICKS.

(See p. 118.)

THE principle of these bricks consists in making the two opposite sides of a brick with a groove or rabbet in the middle. The groove must be a little more than half the width of the side of the brick, to allow room for the mortar. (See fig. 1.)

Fig. 1.

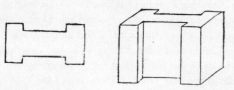

This is the simplest form of these bricks, but the principle will be preserved, though the form of the groove or rabbet may vary, provided the opposite side of the brick vary in proportion, so as to fit together when built into a wall. (See figure 2, where A and B are the two opposite sides of a brick.)

Fig. 2.

A.   B.

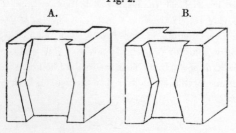

For the purpose of breaking the joints in the depth of the wall, bricks may be made of different lengths, though of the same width. Buildings constructed with these bricks will require no bond timbers, as the walls can neither bulge nor crack without breaking through the bricks themselves.

In applying this principle to arches, the sides of the grooves and the shoulders should be radii of a circle of which the arch is a segment, though if the circle be very large, a minute attention to this point is scarcely neces sary. When the arch is very flat it may be well to have the shoulders dovetailed, to prevent the arch from cracking across, as is seen in figure 3.

Fig. 3.

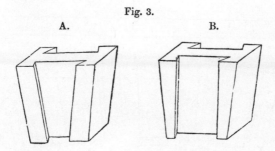

A.   B.

When the bricks are as wide at the bottom as at the top, the manner of dovetailing them is obvious, but when they are wider at the top, the sides of the *shoulders* must be parallel on one side of the brick (Fig. 3, A.) and the side of the *groove* on the other. (B.)

The appearance of the bricks in the face of an upright

wall, and also on both surfaces of an arch (when not dove-tailed) is shewn in figure 4.

Fig. 4.

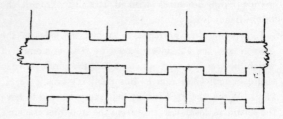

The mode of constructing an arch is shewn in figure 5.

Fig. 5.

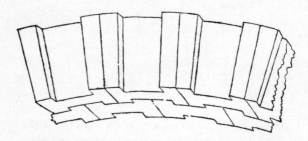

F.

MR. CARTWRIGHT'S PRIZE ESSAY ON MANURES.

(See p. 206.)

With Notes by Sir Humphry Davy.

THERE are few arts of practical application in which more experiments have been tried than in agriculture. In that department of it which relates to the article of manures alone, they have been almost innumerable. The theories on which they have been founded, or have given rise to, have been nearly as numerous as the experiments themselves. Yet it will be admitted, that the experiments on manures have not been hitherto so diversified as the nature of the subject might demand; their object being, for the most part, merely confined to the comparison of one manure with another. The result of such experiments often proves very fallacious, from the manner in which each respective manure produces its effects not being taken into consideration, and by not adverting to the peculiarities of the different soils on which they might have been tried. Hence a manure which under one set of experiments is found to be valuable, under another is condemned as useless; and that which is esteemed useless by the first experimenter, in the hands of the next is considered as the reverse. This benefit, however, has arisen from these experiments, imperfectly conducted as they have been: they furnish reasonable data for estimating the quantum of one manure as equivalent to the quantum of another of the same class, so as to make it a matter of mere pecuniary calculation, according to local circumstances, which is to be preferred.

There are many facts yet to be ascertained respecting the nature of manures, on which the general opinion is by no means agreed; and even from those facts which are already ascertained, the conclusions are not always uniform.

This uncertainty seems in part to have arisen from not considering the manner in which the different substances used as manures act under different circumstances. Were all substances so used, the immediate food of plants, their operation, in proportion to the quantity of nutriment which each substance might afford, would, under all circumstances of variation of soil, be nearly the same; but this we find is by no means the case. Hence the conclusion is, that there are substances used as manures whose beneficial effects proceed from other causes than the mere furnishing sustenance to the growing vegetable. To investigate these causes has been the object of the experiments detailed in this essay. As there has been no set of experiments, as far as I know, for the express purpose of elucidating this view of the subject, familiar as the ideas it suggests are to every one who has paid any attention to the philosophy of manures, I thought I might render some small service at least to the cause of agriculture by stating them.

The substances employed as manures are, mineral, vegetable, and animal, or animalized matter:* of these,

---

* I do not know that animalized matter is different from animal matter.—H. D.

some appear to produce their effects chiefly, if not altogether, by their mechanical operation on the soil itself, by altering its texture; others, by their chemical agency on the different substances contained in the soil; others, by furnishing nutriment or stimulus to the assimilating or (if I may so express myself) the digestive organs of the plants themselves.

The method which I have adopted, as being that which appeared the most obvious for arriving at the deductions I was in pursuit of, has been, first, to try the manures in each class separately, which might furnish the opportunity of remarking their simple operation, and then to use them in combination, from whence might be deduced their chemical influence on each other.

The mineral substances I have employed are — lime, gypsum, sulphuric acid, and common salt.

The vegetable substances are—peat, peat-ashes, woodashes, decayed leaves, saw-dust, malt-dust, alkaline salts, and (though not strictly in all cases a vegetable production) soot.

The animal substances are—bone-dust and chandlers' graves. The animalized matters are stable and fold-yard dung. The vegetable and animal, or animalized matters, that might have been used as manures, are almost infinite; but as I consider them as respectively the same in their component parts, only varying as one or other component part may chance to be more or less concentrated, and to predominate, I confined myself to such as can be most easily obtained.

Having appropriated half an acre to each set of experiments, I divided it into sixty equal parts, which were manured (the first excepted) as follows :—

No.	Quantities.	No.	
1.	No manure.	28.	Lime, sulphuric acid, salt.
2.	Sulphuric acid - 3 oz.	29.	Lime, salt, peat.
3.	Sea-salt - - - ¼ peck.	30.	Lime, salt, dung.
4.	Lime - - - - 1 bush.	31.	Lime, peat, dung.
5.	Gypsum - - - ¼ peck.	32.	Lime, salt, gypsum, peat
6.	Soot - - - - 1 peck.	33.	Gypsum, dung.
7.	Wood-ashes - - 2 pecks.	34.	Gypsum, peat.
8.	Saw-dust - - 3 bush.	35.	Gypsum, graves.
9.	Malt-dust - - 2 pecks.	36.	Gypsum, bone-dust.
10.	Peat - - - - 3 bush.	37.	Gypsum, wood-ashes.
11.	Decayed leaves - 3 bush.	38.	Gypsum, leaves.
12.	Fresh dung - - 3 bush.	39.	Soot, dung.
13.	Rotted dung - 1 bush.	40.	Soot, peat.
14.	Bone-dust - - 1 peck.	41.	Soot, salt.
15.	Chandlers' graves, 9 lb.	42.	Wood-ashes, dung.
16.	Lime, sulphuric acid.*	43.	Wood-ashes, peat.
17.	Lime, sea-salt.	44.	Wood-ashes, salt.
18.	Lime, soot.	45.	Wood-ashes, decayed leaves.
19.	Lime, wood-ashes.		
20.	Lime, saw-dust.	46.	Wood-ashes, bone-dust.
21.	Lime, malt-dust.	47.	Wood-ashes, malt-dust.
22.	Lime, peat.	48.	Saw-dust, dung.
23.	Lime, leaves.	49.	Saw-dust, salt.
24.	Lime, dung.	50.	Malt-dust, salt.
25.	Lime, bone-dust.	51.	Peat, dung.
26.	Lime, chandlers' graves.	52.	Peat, salt.
27.	Lime, pond-mud.	53.	Peat, decayed leaves.

* In this and the following numbers the quantities of each ingredient are the same as when used singly.

No.
54. Peat, bone-dust, salt.
55. Decayed leaves, salt.
56. Decayed leaves, dung.
57. Peat-ashes, dung.

No.
58. Peat-ashes, salt.
59. Peat-ashes, lime.
60. Chandlers' graves, salt.*

On the 14th of April, 1804, the whole was planted with potatoes; and that the experiment might be conducted with all possible accuracy, each part received the same number of sets. On the 14th of May, a few days after the plants appeared, No. 9, malt-dust, was perceptibly the most vigorous, next to which, in succession, were the following :—

No.
15. Chandlers' graves.
26. Lime, chandlers' graves.
21. Lime, malt-dust.
34. Gypsum, peat.
35. Gypsum, chandlers' graves.
40. Soot, peat.
47. Wood-ashes, malt-dust.
32. Lime, salt, gypsum, peat.
60. Chandlers' graves, salt.
50. Malt-dust, salt.
11. Decayed leaves.
6. Soot.
5. Gypsum.
3. Salt.
2. Sulphuric acid.

No.
1. No manure.
7. Wood-ashes.
10. Peat.
13. Rotted dung.
14. Bone-dust.
16. Lime, sulphuric acid.
18. Lime, soot.
22. Lime, peat.
23. Lime, decayed leaves.
25. Lime, bone-dust.
27. Lime, pond-mud.
28. Lime, sulphuric acid, salt.
24. Lime, dung.
31. Lime, peat, dung.
36. Gypsum, bone-dust.

* I am sorry to see metallic matters omitted; such as green vitriol, or sulphate of iron; oxyde of iron, or ochre, &c.—H. D.

No.		No.	
37.	Gypsum, wood-ashes.	4.	Lime.
38.	Gypsum.	8.	Saw-dust.
39.	Soot, dung.	12.	Fresh dung.
41.	Soot, salt.	17.	Lime, salt.
42.	Wood-ashes, dung.	19.	Lime, wood-ashes.
43.	Wood-ashes, peat.	20.	Lime, saw-dust.
44.	Wood-ashes, salt.	24.	Lime, dung.
45.	Wood-ashes, decayed leaves.	30.	Lime, salt, dung.
		33.	Gypsum, dung.
46.	Wood-ashes, bone-dust.	48.	Saw-dust, dung.
51.	Peat, dung.	56.	Decayed leaves, dung.
52.	Peat, salt.	57.	Peat-ashes, dung.
53.	Peat, decayed leaves.	58.	Peat-ashes, salt.
54.	Peat, bone-dust, salt.	59.	Peat-ashes, lime.
55.	Decayed leaves, salt.	49.	Saw-dust, salt.

It will be necessary here to observe, that from No. 9 to No. 3 inclusive, the gradation of excellence was obviously perceptible. From No. 2 to No. 55 inclusive, there was little or no perceptible difference. From No. 4 to No. 49 the plants were considerably inferior to those included in No. 2 and No. 55.

It is worthy of remark that, in this stage of the business, the experiment is in favour of malt-dust, soot, and graves; and the reason why it is so seems to be apparent. Sugar,* mucilage,† and carbon,‡ being the principal in-

* I should say, because saccharine matter is probably more nutritious than any other vegetable matter, or than any animal matter.—H. D.

† Chandlers' graves, I suppose, are beneficial because the mucilage is in the fittest state for speedy or immediate absorption.—H. D.

‡ This experiment seems to shew, what has not been done

gredients and constituent parts in the composition of
vegetables, it is natural to suppose that those substances
which are most readily disposed to putrefy, or which present themselves in a state of the nearest assimilation to the
plant which is to be fed by them, will be more immediately
imbibed than such as must previously be decomposed
either by their own internal fermentation or by the action
of external causes.

On the 28th of May, the apparent vigour of the plants
was in the following order :—

9. Malt-dust. 15. Chandlers' graves. 26. Lime, chandlers'
graves. 21. Lime, malt-dust. 40. Soot, peat. 47. Wood-
ashes, malt-dust. 13. Rotted dung. 6. Soot. 18. Lime, soot.
59. Peat, bone-dust. 10. Peat. 31. Lime, peat, dung. 32.
Lime, salt, gypsum, peat. 34. Gypsum, peat. 35. Gypsum,
chandlers'. graves. 36. Gypsum, bone-dust. 37. Gypsum,
wood-ashes. 38. Gypsum, leaves. 39. Soot, dung. 41. Soot,
salt. 43. Wood-ashes, peat. 46. Wood-ashes, bone-dust.
50. Malt-dust, salt. 51. Peat, dung. 52. Peat, salt. 53,
Peat, decayed leaves. 55. Decayed leaves, salt. 60. Chandlers' graves, salt. 1. No manure. 2. Sulphuric acid. 3. Salt.
5. Gypsum. 7. Wood-ashes. 11. Decayed leaves. 14. Bone-
dust. 19. Lime, wood-ashes. 22. Lime, peat. 23. Lime, decayed leaves. 25. Lime, bone-dust. 27. Lime, pond-mud.
28. Lime, sulphuric acid, salt. 29. Lime, salt, peat. 33.
Gypsum, dung. 42. Wood-ashes, dung. 44. Wood-ashes,
salt. 45. Wood-ashes, decayed leaves. 58. Peat-ashes, salt.

before,—that carbon in the state of a subtle powder, as in the
sublimate called soot, is really absorbed with facility, and
accordingly either nourishes or stimulates more speedily.—
H. D.

12. Fresh dung. 4. Lime. 54. Peat, bone-dust, salt. 57. Peat-ashes, dung. 56. Decayed leaves, dung. 49. Saw-dust, salt. 48. Saw-dust, dung. 20. Lime, saw-dust. 30. Lime, salt, dung. 24. Lime, dung. 17. Lime, salt. 16. Lime, sulphuric acid. 8. Saw-dust.

The variations between this table and the former are worthy of observation. In the first table, sixteen of the experiments take place of No. 1, in this, twenty-eight have the superiority. The same reason which is applied to the former table may assist us in accounting for the results of this. The different manures beginning now to develop themselves, and to be decomposed, give out (though as yet in moderate proportion) the requisite aliment to the plants they are to sustain.

On the 2nd of July, Nos. 26 and 21 had taken the lead of No. 9; and on the 24th of the same month No. 35 had visibly outstripped them all.

On the 21st of September, when the roots were taken up, the order of precedence was as follows:—

No.		Produce.
35.	Gypsum, graves - - - - -	250 lbs.
41.	Soot, salt - - - - - -	240
21.	Lime, malt-dust - - - - -	239
18.	Lime, soot - - - - - -	231
39.	Soot, dung - - - - - -	228
40.	Soot, peat - - - - - -	225
34.	Gypsum, peat - - - - -	222
15.	Graves - - - - - -	220
26.	Lime, graves - - - - -	219
44.	Wood-ashes, salt - - - - -	219

No.		Produce.
37.	Gypsum, wood-ashes - - - -	218 lbs.
43.	Wood-ashes, peat - - - - -	217
16.	Lime, sulphuric acid - - - -	213
45.	Wood-ashes, decayed leaves - -	213
47.	Wood-ashes, malt-dust - - - -	213
42.	Wood-ashes, dung - - - -	210
46.	Wood-ashes, bone-dust - - - -	208
33.	Gypsum, dung - - - -	207
36.	Gypsum, bone-dust - - -	206
38.	Gypsum, dry leaves - - -	205
13.	Rotted dung - - - -	201
32.	Lime, salt, gypsum, peat - - -	201
30.	Lime, salt, dung - - - -	199
3.	Salt - - - - - -	198
56.	Decayed leaves, dung - - -	198
60.	Graves, salt - - - - -	195
31.	Lime, peat, dung - - - -	194
14.	Bone-dust - - - - -	193
6.	Soot - - - - - -	192
12.	Fresh dung - - - - -	192
25.	Lime, bone-dust - - - -	190
50.	Malt-dust, salt - - - -	189
24.	Lime, dung - - - - -	188
7.	Wood-ashes - - - - -	187
55	Decayed leaves, salt - - -	187
19.	Lime, wood-ashes - - -	185
58.	Peat-ashes, salt - - - -	185
9.	Malt-dust - - - -	184
29.	Lime, salt, peat - - - -	183
51.	Peat, dung - - - - -	183
57.	Peat-ashes, dung - - - -	183
48.	Saw-dust, dung - - - -	180

No.							Produce.
49.	Saw-dust, salt	-	-	-	-	-	180 lbs.
22.	Lime, peat -	-	-	-	-	-	179
5.	Gypsum	-	-	-	-	-	178
54.	Peat, bone-dust	-	-	-	-	-	178
11.	Decayed leaves	-	-	-	-		175
28.	Lime, sulphuric acid, salt	-	-	-			175
53.	Peat, decayed leaves	-	-	-	-		172
23.	Lime, decayed leaves	-	-	-	-		171
52.	Peat, salt	-	-	-	-	-	171
59.	Peat-ashes, lime	-	-	-	-	-	171
2.	Sulphuric acid	-	-	-	-	-	170
17.	Lime, salt	-	-	-	-	-	167
20.	Lime, saw-dust	-	-	-	-	-	166
10.	Peat -	-	-	-	-	-	159
1.	No manure -	-	-	-	-	-	157
8.	Saw-dust	-	-	-	-	-	155
4.	Lime -	-	-	-	-	-	150
27.	Lime, pond-mud	-	-	-	-	-	150

The final result of these experiments not only tends to ascertain some doubtful facts, but leads, it is presumed, to some important conclusions.

The first article used as manure is sulphuric acid. The use of this substance was first suggested, if I mistake not, by the late ingenious Dr. G. Fordyce; whether it ever was brought to the test of experiment, I am not able to ascertain. It appears, however, that its effects are beneficial; but whether those effects are produced by its assisting in the decomposition* of animal or vegetable matter in the soil, by stimulating the organs of the plant, or by supplying it with oxygen, are questions which I

* Not by decompounding but by stimulating.—H. D.

will not take upon me to answer. Dr. George Fordyce, if I remember right, leans to the latter opinion.*

In experiment No. 16, where the sulphuric acid is combined with lime, my object was to try the effect of an artificial gypsum, in which, however, the lime very much predominated. A reference to the foregoing table will shew that it may be used with considerable efficacy. The expense of gypsum in many parts of the kingdom, remote from where it is found, admitting not of its being applied to agricultural purposes, it occurred to me that a factitious gypsum might be a valuable succedaneum.

In experiment No. 28, the sulphuric acid being diluted with a sufficient quantity of water, and the salt mixed with it, the whole was thrown upon the unslaked lime; by this commixture of sulphuric acid and salt, I was of opinion that the marine acid would fly off, leaving the soda; and that the heat and effervescence excited by slaking the lime might possibly assist in the operation.

If we compare this experiment with No. 4, it certainly is not without a beneficial effect; but whether in consequence of the expulsion of marine acid, it may be difficult to determine.

Opinions have been long divided on the subject of sea-salt as a manure. From this set of experiments, at least, there is reason to conclude it possesses considerable activity. It is matter of observation, that in thirteen different combinations of salt with other substances, four only are superior to salt used alone—namely, No. 32,

* His experiments with sulphuric acid will be found among the papers of the Board of Agriculture during the reign of Sinclair.—H. D.

41, 30, and 44; and in eight out of thirteen the salt added to the efficacy of the matters combined with it;—as, for example,

No.		Produce.
4. Lime alone gives - - - - -		150 lbs.
Combined with salt, No. 17, the produce is		167
	Superiority - - ——	17
22. Lime and peat give - - -		179
29. Ditto, with the addition of salt		183
	Superiority - - ——	4
6. Soot - - - - - -		192
41. Soot and salt - - - - -		270
	Superiority - - ——	48
44. Wood-ashes and salt - - -		219
7. Wood-ashes - - - - -		187
	Superiority - - ——	32
8. Saw-dust - - - - -		155
49. Saw-dust and salt - - - -		180
	Superiority - - ——	25
9. Malt-dust - - - - -		184
50. Malt-dust and salt - - - -		189
	Superiority - - ——	5
11. Decayed leaves - - - -		175
55. Decayed leaves and salt - - -		187
	Superiority - - ——	12
24. Lime and dung - - - -		188
30. Lime, dung, and salt - - -		199
	Superiority - - ——	11

In four instances, the salt appears to have done harm:

16. Artificial gypsum - - - -		213
28. Artificial gypsum and salt - -		175
	Superiority - - ——	38

No.						Produce.
16. Artificial gypsum	-	-	-	-	-	213 lbs.
32. Lime, peat, gypsum, and salt	-	-	-	201
		Superiority	-	-	—— 12
14. Bone-dust	-	-	-	-	-	193
54. Bone-dust and salt	-	-	-	-	178
		Superiority	-	-	—— 15
15. Graves	-	-	-	-	-	220
60. Graves and salt	-	-	-	-	195
		Superiority	-	-	—— 25

In the two last of the above experiments, possibly the antiseptic quality of the salt might retard the putrefactive process, so as to render the bone-dust and graves less efficacious than they would have been had the salt been omitted.

Were I to hazard a conjecture on the general good effect of salt in these experiments, I should attribute it, in a considerable degree, to its property of attracting moisture; for I observed that those parts of the field where the salt was applied were for a considerable time visibly moister than the rest,—I mean, so long as the dry weather continued; after the rains fell, that distinction, of course, was obliterated.

But in none of these experiments have theory and practice been so at variance as in the application of lime and its different combinations. The general good effect with which lime is applied led me to expect that, though the simple application of it might not prove strikingly beneficial, yet combined with other manures, and those so different in their qualities, its effects could not but be obvious.

No. 4, lime alone, and No. 27, combined with pond-mud, are the least productive. In sixteen experiments it does not appear to have been particularly efficacious, except in four instances ; when applied by itself, it does harm rather than good, producing only 150 lb. The produce of No. 27, when mixed with the pond-mud, is the same. This latter fact is rather curious.* The soil on which the experiment was tried was a loose ferruginous sand, but was brought to its present texture by a very thick covering of pond mud ; so that it received no accession of fertility by the additional quantity that was given to it, nor did the lime meet with anything to operate upon in that additional quantity, which was not in the soil before.

Gypsum, though used with great success on the Continent and in America, has not hitherto been considered as a very efficacious manure by the English farmer. My experiments, however, induce me to think very favourably of it, especially when combined with other substances.

No.		Produce.
5. Gypsum - - - - -	-	178 lbs.
1. No manure - - - - -	-	157
Superiority -	-	—— 21
32. Lime, salt, peat, and gypsum -	-	201
29. Lime, salt, and peat - -	-	183
Superiority -	-	—— 18
33. Gypsum, dung - - - -	-	207
12. Dung - - - - -	-	192
Superiority -	-	—— 15

* Probably the mud was little else than clay or sandy matter ; and if so, would be harmful.—H. D.

No.		Produce.
39.	Gypsum and peat - - - - -	222 lbs.
10.	Peat - - - - - - -	159
	Superiority - - —— 63
35.	Gypsum and graves - - -	250
15.	Graves - - - - - -	220
	Superiority - - —— 30
36.	Gypsum and bone-dust - - -	206
14.	Bone-dust - - - - -	193
	Superiority - - —— 13
37.	Gypsum and wood-ashes - - -	218
7.	Wood-ashes - - - - -	187
	Superiority - - —— 31
38.	Gypsum and dried leaves, not decayed	205
11.	Decayed leaves - - - -	175
	Superiority - - —— 30

To these instances we may add No. 16, factitious gypsum.

The most striking of these experiments is No. 35; and it is to be remarked, in general, that previous to the middle of July, the plants where the gypsum had been used gave no indication of superiority; their subsequent vigour can be accounted for on no other ground than on the supposition that the septic quality of the gypsum had not, till then, produced its effects in the decomposition of the substances (the wood-ashes excepted) which the gypsum was combined with.*

* Or that the gypsum impeded the absorption of the mucilage in the graves, although it continued to stimulate; for in this case we had two kinds of manures—viz., a stimulating and a nutritious one.—H. D.

Of soot, the most remarkable circumstance is its efficacy in combination with salt, in experiment 41, and this efficacy I am disposed to attribute to a property in salt taken notice of before—namely, its attraction of moisture ; a property which could not fail of being beneficial when the salt was combined with so hot and dry a manure as soot, which, from its acrid nature, requires to be much diluted.

It was expected that wood-ashes, from the power which alkaline salts have of decomposing animal and vegetable matter, would have been more efficacious than they appear to have been by these experiments. By referring, however, to the foregoing table, it will be seen that they have in no instance been applied without efficacy.

The article of which I had the greatest doubt was saw-dust, from its known effect of destroying weeds when spread tolerably thick on gravel walks. In the first stages, indeed, of the business, it was very unpromising. The plants at first were very backward and sickly; by degrees, however, they recovered themselves, which I attributed to the acid, or tanning principle in the saw-dust being spent or washed out by the subsequent rains. That the saw-dust, even after it had lost its tanning principle, should have no material operation on the soil the first year is not to be wondered at, as the carbon, which is its principal ingredient, will remain for some time in a state of great insolubility. There can be little doubt of its effects being very apparent at a future season.

It will be seen, by referring to the former tables, that malt-dust is very immediate in its operations; but from the last table it would appear that its effects are not so permanent as some other manures of slower dissolution, and which require longer time before they can be decomposed and become soluble in water.

Though malt-dust may possess no durable property, yet its immediate and powerful operation in promoting a rapid vegetation points it out as a valuable manure, especially when it can be used as a top-dressing to plants in an advanced state of growth. In this mode I have used it, in a set of experiments unconnected with the present, with the greatest success, applying it to the potato crop immediately before earthing up.

The peat in the part of the country where these experiments are tried containing a considerable proportion of oxyde of iron, I was not very sanguine in my expectations of any very powerful effect from it, in whatever form it might be applied, on a soil of which the iron it already contains constitutes about a fifty-seventh part. Leaves, in a state of imperfect decay, bearing no very remote resemblance to peat in its simple state, uncombined with iron or sulphur, I wished to compare them together. I had, however, another object in view in introducing leaves into the experiment, which was, to recommend a practice, too much neglected, of collecting them in the autumn, (when it can be conveniently done,) either to be laid in a heap to ferment and rot, or to be mixed with dung; or which, perhaps, is a better way still, to furnish litter for the fold-yard, mixing with them a due proportion of straw or stubble. When singly applied, the advantage in this experiment is in favour of decayed leaves; in combination with other substances, they appear nearly upon a par.

It is usually calculated that three, if not four, loads of

fresh dung from the fold-yard will be required to make one load after the dung has undergone the putrefactive process. I wished, therefore, to institute a comparison between them in these two different stages, with a view to ascertain the advantage or disadvantage of the usual method of not laying on dung till it is completely or nearly rotted. In this comparison I tried only three bushels of fresh dung against one of rotted dung.

No.	Produce.
13. Rotted dung* - - - - - - -	201 lbs.
12. Fresh dung - - - - - -	192
Superiority in favour of rotted dung - ——	9

The experiment, however, does not terminate here: their comparative effects must be pursued through subsequent seasons till the soil requires to be renovated afresh. It is reasonable to conclude that the dung which is now laid on fresh will continue its efficacy after the rotted dung is exhausted.

Dung combined with soot, No. 39; with wood-ashes, No. 42; and with gypsum, No. 33, seems to have been benefited by the combination; but its greatest effects are to be looked for in the succeeding crop.

Bone-dust being of difficult dissolution, it was natural to suppose its effects would be considerably augmented by combination with such substances as would assist in its decomposition. The justice of this opinion will appear by

* It must be a most wasteful custom to keep dung till it is further putrefied, because the sole use of the putrefactive process is to break down the texture to fit the matter for dissolution and absorption, in which state fresh dung is already. Straw is not so; it should be rotted; so should saw-dust.— H. D.

comparing the effect of bone-dust when used by itself, and
when in combination with gypsum, or wood-ashes.*

No.					Produce.
36. Bone-dust and gypsum	-	-	-	-	206 lbs.
14. Bone-dust	-	-	-	-	193
Superiority	-	-	—— 13
46. Wood-ashes and bone-dust	-	-	-	208
7. Wood-ashes	-	-	-	-	187
Superiority	-	-	—— 21

Bones are a manure as efficacious as permanent, and
consequently they should be collected wherever they are
to be met with—a practice, however, which is never
attended to by the farmer, except in situations where
there are mills for grinding them.

Of the same nature with bone-dust are chandlers'
graves; but from their more rapid tendency to become
putrid and soluble in water, their operation as manure is
also more rapid.

Of the fifteen simple manures, chandlers' graves stand
first, as they do also in combination; though soot, in combination, is scarcely inferior.

The operation of every manure must, in a greater or less
degree, be influenced by the quality of the soil on which
it is applied. That every possible light may be thrown
on the subject of these experiments, I have subjoined an
analysis of the soil on which they were tried.† Four

* The superiority was from the stimulating quality of the
gypsum and wood-ashes.—H. D.

† These analyses were made by Sir H. Davy, as appears
from the letters between him and Mr. Cartwright, at p. 206.
—EDITOR.

hundred grains gave of siliceous sand of different degrees of fineness about—

	Grains.
	280
Of finely divided matter, which appeared in the form of clay - - - - - - - -	104
Loss in water - - - - - - - -	16
	400

The 104 grains of finely-divided matter contained

Of carbonate of lime - - - - - - -	18
Oxyde of iron - - - - - - - -	7
Loss by incineration, most probably from vegetable decomposing matter - - - - -	17

Remainder principally silex and alumine. There was no indication of gypsum or phosphate of lime.

This analysis accounts, not unsatisfactorily, for two at least of the phenomena in the foregoing experiments— namely, the great activity of gypsum, and the inutility of peat-ashes. The soil, containing in itself no gypsum, receives from the application of that mineral an accession of active power which it wanted; and having already more than a necessary share of iron in its composition, it becomes, by the addition of peat-ashes, supersaturated with that which in certain proportions is an invigorating stimulant, but when too abundant, operates as a poison.

Two sets of experiments, and with the same proportion of manures, were tried, on a soil of a very different nature, with buck-wheat and turnips. As my object in these two sets of experiments was to try the intrinsic effects of manures, unaided by any vegetating principle in the soil, I chose the poorest I could meet with. Of its poverty judgment may be made by the following analysis :—

	Grains.
400 grains gave, of siliceous sand - - -	320
Of finely divided matter, which appeared as brown mould - - - - - - -	68
Loss in water - - - - - - -	12
	400

The finely divided matter lost nearly half its weight by incineration, which shews that it contained a great deal of vegetable matter. The residuum was principally a mixture of aluminous and siliceous earths, coloured red by oxyde of iron, and containing very little calcareous matter. There was no indication of either gypsum or phosphate of lime.

The detail of these experiments will be short.

July 6th, 1804, I sowed one piece with turnips, the other with buck-wheat. On the 26th of the same month, each piece was examined minutely. Nos. 1, 2, 3, 5, 6, 7, 8, 9, 14, 49, 50, 54, 58, 60, shewed little or no marks of vegetation. The rest were only in the seed leaf. On the 16th of August, one-half of the turnips and about two-thirds of the buck-wheat were dead. From that period to the 15th of September, after a few alternations of health and sickness, the turnips all died away, except Nos. 12, 18, 21, 24, 25, 26, 30, 35, 39, 42, 47, 56.

On these experiments I have to observe, generally, that where the manures made use of, whether stimulant or nutritive, (as, for instance, salt or malt-dust, did not contribute in some degree to the texture and consistence of the soil, the plants scarcely got into the seed leaf; and that what little health and vigour they afterwards possessed seemed to depend more on the texture and consistence which the soil acquired from the respective manures, than on any other circumstance. Hence the beneficial effects of lime on these soils, as also of clay and argillaceous marls.

It may not be foreign to the purpose of this essay to observe, that adjoining to the piece where these experiments were tried is a field of the same original quality, which within these few years has been reclaimed from a state of nature, and brought into a state of cultivation and fertility, chiefly by improving its texture by a thick coat of marly clay.

Enough has been said, it is presumed, in the detail of the foregoing experiments, to shew the general nature and properties of manures. Respecting their application, I have to observe, that the circumstance of most importance to attend to is the texture of the soil; where it is too loose, such manures should be applied as will add as much as possible to its solidity and consistence, such as marly clay, lime, thoroughly digested dung, graves, or any other unctuous and fertilizing substance which is of little bulk, and which, when reduced to its first principles by decomposition, will not increase the openness and porosity of the soil.

For stronger soils I should recommend, not only semi-digested dung, but dung or litter even in as fresh a state as it could conveniently be applied. Decayed leaves, also, are an excellent manure for strong land; being of very slow dissolution, when once mixed with the soil it is a long time before they permit it to resume its natural tenacity. Lime, also, is beneficially applied to strong as well as light land; being more open in its texture and less adhesive than clay, and less open in its texture and more adhesive than sand, it is applied with equal benefit to soils of either description. I am speaking now merely of its mechanical agency, but of all ameliorating applications to strong land, perhaps sand is the best. The reason is too obvious to insist upon.

Besides a general knowledge of the nature and properties of the manures he employs, the farmer should also be acquainted with the component parts of the soil he intends they should operate upon; otherwise he may be in danger of aggravating its defects, or, at least, wasting his efforts to no purpose.

As a general rule it may be observed, that no mineral manure should be applied to a soil abounding in the same mineral already. As mineral manures appear to operate more by their chemical agency than in any other way, their principal use seems to be to correct and neutralize what is noxious in the original composition of the soil, and to assist in the decomposition of those substances which, in their present state of insolubility, are useless.

For the purpose of preparing fold or stable manure for the field, it has been proposed to manufacture it (if I may so express myself) under covered buildings, with a view of defending it from the influence of the elements. In this there is certainly more of refinement than practical utility. Add to this the inconvenience of having to carry the manure perhaps a mile or two, at a time when, if it were even laid in the very field where it is wanted, the farmer can hardly find time to spread it before the seed ought to be in the ground.

It is needless to dwell upon the expensiveness of this plan. Landlords already find the providing and keeping in repair such buildings as are of unavoidable necessity a tax sufficiently heavy, without incumbering themselves with others, which, perhaps, their tenants would not thank them for.

The most advantageous, and in the end, perhaps the cheapest way, is, to form the dunghill, or compost heap, as near to the field where it is to be used as conveniently may be. It is true, more labour is required in the first instance; but labour is of different value at different seasons. The farmer can better appropriate four days, at some seasons of the year, to the leading his dung from the fold-yard to the field, that it may be ready against the time it is wanted, than he can spare one day in the hurry of seed time.

In forming a dunghill, it is of more importance than is commonly imagined to mix a certain portion of soil with it. When dung is formed into a heap by itself, it is exposed on all sides to the rain and to the exhaling influence of the sun and wind ; by mixing and covering it with soil, these inconveniences may in a great measure be prevented. But this is not all ; a dunghill thrown up in a common way loses, by unavoidable drainage and evaporation, a greater proportion of its fertilizing principles than can be well calculated. What it loses by drainage is, indeed, obvious to the eye ; and it is easy to conceive what it must lose by evaporation, by only observing the steam which is perpetually rising from it during its fermentation. But when soil is mixed with it, the drainage is prevented, and the gaseous fluid and volatile alkali, which would otherwise fly off, are prevented from escaping; or, if they quit the dunghill, are absorbed and retained by the soil.

To ascertain how far soil, when only laid upon a dunghill, absorbs and retains those fertilizing principles which would otherwise be lost in the atmosphere, I took from an old hot-bed, which had been employed through the winter in forcing asparagus, as much soil as would fill a trench one foot deep and six feet square. From the same heap of earth whence this soil was taken, but which had been fallow through the winter, I filled another trench of the same dimensions. I planted the two with lettuces, all, as nearly as possible, of equal size and vigour. When full grown, I drew and weighed them. The produce of the first trench was 42 lb.; of the latter, 33 lb. If the increased fertility of soil is so great from merely lying on the surface of a dunghill, what must it be when generally mixed with it? To this it may perhaps be objected, that by mixing soil with dung you impede or retard its fermentation. This, however, ought to be no objection; unless the farmer is hurried in point of time, as dung cannot ferment too slowly.

In forming a compost heap, the farmer cannot bring together too many or too discordant ingredients, as they will all mutually assist in the decomposition of each other. Amongst other articles, I particularly recommend bones, unless where there is a bone-mill. These should be laid in the middle of the heap, where the fermentation is greatest. When the heap is removed, the bones are to

R

be taken out and put into the next compost heap that may be made, as they will undergo a partial dissolution in every heap which they are put into; each heap will, as far as that dissolution goes, be benefited by them, till at length the bones are totally dissolved.

Before I conclude this essay, it may be necessary to observe, that it has been my endeavour (and in which I am willing to hope I have succeeded) to express myself in such terms as to be intelligible, not only to the theoretical and scientific, but to the mere practical farmer. I have endeavoured also to avoid, as much as possible, indulging in theory and hypothesis. Though the inferences which I have occasionally drawn seem warranted by the facts that have presented themselves, yet are they offered with the greatest diffidence. Sensible of the uncertainty attendant on experiments, liable not only to the influence of latent, and perhaps inscrutable, causes in the element in which they have been tried, but subject also to every variation of the atmosphere, it would have been rashness and presumption to have spoken with absolute decision on points which possibly may yet require many years, if not ages, to determine.

G.

MANCHESTER MEMORIAL, AUGUST, 1807.

(See p. 222.)

To His Grace the Duke of Portland, First Lord, and the other Lords Commissioners of his Majesty's Treasury.

The Memorial of the undersigned inhabitants of the town and neighbourhood of Manchester,

Sheweth,—

That the great advantages which have arisen to this country from the increase of its manufactures, and the consequent extension of its commerce, have been chiefly derived from the application of the powers of water and steam to the operations of spinning and weaving, which before were performed by the slow, expensive, and less effectual strength of man.

That the Reverend Edmund Cartwright, D.D., by his various useful inventions to render the process of weaving practicable by the above powers, as well as by his machines for combing wool, and other mechanical inventions for the improvement of British manufactures, has rendered most essential services to this country.

That the continued application of Dr. Cartwright to the discovery and improvement of these inventions, has not only deprived him of the pecuniary advantages which he might have derived from them, but has caused him to expend a large private fortune in bringing to perfection his valuable inventions.

That, under these circumstances, your Memorialists humbly hope that Government will be pleased to reward his important services with some substantial mark of their favour and the gratitude of the country.

Peter Marsland.
Samuel Oldknow.
John Marsland.
Hen. and J. Barton & Co.
B. H. Green.
John Fisher.
Nathaniel Gould.
Samuel Greg.
Peter Ewart.
J. Jackson.
Richard Rushford.
J. Gill.
W. Potter.
Roger Holland.
Horrocks & Co., Preston.
J. Watson & Sons, Preston.
Paul Cotterall and Co., Preston.
Sidgreaves, Leighton, and Co., Preston.
Riley, Paley, & Co. Preston.
Robert and W. Jarrett.
Ottiwell Wood.
John Lowe.
Josephus Smith.
Thomas Tipping.
James Heald.
Henry Fielding & Brothers.
William Starkie.
G. Philips.
John Atkinson.
John Close.
Thomas Drinkwater.
Ch. Fred. Brand & Co.
R. and J. Jackson.
Charles Wood & Co.
Samuel Peel.
James Touchet.
Joshua Barnsley.
William Mitchell.
Entwistles & Steirtivant.
W. Myers and Nephew.
Joseph Siddon, borough-reeve of Manchester.

H.

LIST OF DR. CARTWRIGHT'S PATENTS.

1. A machine for weaving, April 4, 1785.
2. Improvements in the same, October 30, 1786.
3. Further improvements, August 1, 1787.
4. Further improvements, November 13, 1788.
5. Wool-combing machine, August 22, 1789.
6. Further improvements in wool-combing, April 27, 1790.
7. Further improvements, December 11, 1790.
8. For manufacturing wool, hemp, flax, &c., into yarn, twist, ropes, &c., May 15, 1792.
9. Improvement in the form of bricks, April 14, 1795.
10. Incombustible material for dwelling-houses, October 11, 1797.
11. Steam-engine, November 11, 1797.
12. Improvements in steam-engines, February 5, 1801.

INDEX.

ERRATA.

Page 5, line 11, *for* Ayho,   *read* Aynho.

    10, —   6, — four,   — five.

    74, — 11, — in which, — and in the evidence before parliament.

    98, — 14, — 25th,   — 15th.

  103, — 17, — nine,   — eight.

  193, — 16, — effect,   — affect.